Jacqueline Kennedy Onassis

1929-1994

Charles Lawliss

JG PRESS

Published by
JG Press, a Trademark of JG Press, Inc.
Distributed by
World Publications, Inc.
455 Somerset Avenue
North Dighton, MA 02764

Produced by JG Press, Inc.
and Wieser & Wieser, Inc.
118 East 25th Street
New York, NY 10010

ISBN 1-57215-040-8

Printed in the United States of America

Photo Credits
UPI/BETTMANN: 4, 6, 7, 8 (upper left), 9, 10, 12, 14
(upper & lower), 15, 16, 17 (upper & lower), 18, 19, 20
(upper & lower), 21, 22, 23 (left & right), 24, 26 (upper
& lower), 27 (left & right), 28, 29, 30, 31, 32, 33, 34, 35,
36, 37, 38-39, 40, 42, 44-45, 46, 47, 48-49, 50, 51, 52, 53,
55 (upper & lower), 58-59, 60-61, 62, 63, 64, 65, 66, 67,
68, 69, 70, 71, 72, 73, 74, 76, 77, 78, 79 (upper & lower),
80, 82, 83, 84 (upper), 85, 86, 87, 89, 90, 91, 92 (upper &
lower), 93, 94, 95, 98, 100, 102, 108, 112.
REUTERS/BETTMANN: 81, 84 (lower), 88, 96-97, 101,
104-105, 109, 113, 114-115, 116, 117, 118-119, 120-121,
122-123.
THE BETTMANN ARCHIVE: 8 (lower right), 13, 41,
124-125, 126-127, 128.

Introduction

We were captivated with her. Everyone was in the 1960's. She was beautiful and she dressed beautifully. But it was more than beauty. She was poised, intelligent and elegant. She helped her husband win the Presidency, and along the way they won our hearts. They were our role models. We shared their dreams. It was our Camelot, too.

She was a private person living a public life. Her devotion to her husband and children, her glittering White House soirees, her sense of style, her whispery voice—the stuff of legend. Heads of state clambered to sit next to her, and they hung on her every word.

After the horror of Dallas, her grief was agonizingly public. The image of her standing by her husband's coffin, her suit stained with his blood, is etched in our memory, as if by acid. She became a symbol of courage and hope for a mourning nation. Could she have been only thirty-four years old? Charles de Gaulle, who marched in the funeral procession said: "She gave an example to the whole world of how to behave."

We adopted her after that. We thought she could do no wrong. She was our proof that one can and must go on. When reports of her husband's infidelities tainted his memory, she made us remember his real accomplishments. She would visit his grave every year of her life.

Her marriage to a Greek shipping magnate stunned us. How could she do that? Some said she married him for his money. She ignored the furor and the criticism. We learned that our idol was human, and we learned to live with that knowledge.

After his death she settled down. She was a real mother to her children. She got a job. She worked for worthy causes. She dated. She jogged. She rode horses on weekends. Then she found a man who loved her and she could love. Reporters and photographers still pursued her. She would pass them by, looking straight ahead, smiling stoically.

She wanted nothing more than to grow old gracefully surrounded by the grandchildren she loved so much. To our great sorrow, this was not to be. When she died it broke our hearts.

At her funeral, the President of the United States said, "God gave her very great gifts and imposed upon her great burdens. She bore them all with dignity and grace and uncommon common sense."

Her full name was Jacqueline Lee Bouvier Kennedy Onassis. But she was one of the rare ones, instantly recognizable anywhere in the world by only one name. Jackie.

Mr. and Mrs. John V. Bouvier and their daughter Jacqueline, attend the Sixth Annual Horse Show of the Southhampton Riding and Hunt Club, held August 11, 1934 on the club grounds.

Chapter 1

She arrived five weeks late, on July 28, 1929, in East Hampton, on the south shore of Long Island, where her fashionable parents had gone for the weekend. She weighed eight pounds and had dark fluffy hair, generous lips, a snub nose and beautiful large eyes. She was named Jacqueline ("Jackie") Lee Bouvier after her father, John Vernon Bouvier III, who was called Jack. When she grew up, people would remark on how much she resembled her father.

Her mother, Janet Lee Bouvier, was twenty-two, a slim, attractive brunette. Her father, Jack Bouvier, thirty-eight, was a stockbroker who had been one of New York's most eligible bachelors. He was handsome, tall with shiny black hair and a perpetual suntan and a thirst for riches.

In one way it was a good match. Janet Lee wanted position; the Bouviers were an old Catholic family solidly entrenched in New York society. Jack Bouvier wanted money, the Lees had money. Her grandparents had left Ireland during the potato famine and had prospered in America, and her father owned a bank.

Shortly after the wedding, Jack borrowed money from her family to purchase a seat on the New York Stock Exchange where he became a successful "broker's broker." He prospered but made no attempt to repay the loans. Before he was through, he would borrow even more money from his wife's family.

Another daughter, Caroline Lee, was born to the Bouviers on March 3, 1933. Jack called her Lee and soon everyone did. The family had an estate on Long Island and an elegant eleven-room apartment on Park Avenue in Manhattan. The sisters had a nanny and shared a playroom filled with handmade toys and stuffed animals.

The sisters had quite different personalities. Jackie was bold and outspoken; Lee shy and polite. When Jackie was sent to Miss Chapin's School in Manhattan, her teachers all agreed that though highly intelligent, she was a problem child. She apparently was bored at the exclusive all-girls school, and she didn't want to wear the traditional blue-linen jumper uniform. All of her life Jackie would rebel against regimentation.

In her childhood, Jackie developed a love of horses. She took riding lessons at Miss Chapin's and in the Hamptons during the summer, and soon became an excellent rider, like her mother. She enjoyed riding in competition and, according to a friend, had "a fierce competitive edge." She was so intent on winning, that Lee took a strong dislike to the sport.

While Jackie was learning to ride, her family was falling apart. People were beginning to notice that her mother and father weren't getting along. Neither could live within their means. Jack gambled, on Wall Street and at the racetrack. Janet was ambitious, pushy and materialistic. Angry arguments became common. When trouble loomed, her mother would say to Jackie, "Why don't you go and exercise your pony?"

Jack couldn't leave women alone and seemed to delight in having Janet learn of his peccadilloes. On September 30, 1936, when Jackie was seven, her parents agreed to a six-month trial separation. Jack moved out. He was given weekend visitation rights, and paid $1,050 a month to support Janet and the girls. During the separation, he became a dutiful and indulgent father. When the six months were nearly over, he talked Janet into giving the marriage another chance. It didn't work. All the old troubles resurfaced, and on June 6, 1940, Janet took the girls to Reno, where she obtained a divorce. Jackie adored her father and never really forgave her mother divorcing him.

The emotional impact of the divorce on eleven-year-old Jacqueline Bouvier is described by C. David Heymann in his biography *A Woman Named Jackie*. She was old enough to be aware of the collapse of her world, but too young to absorb its full significance.

Instinctively she blocked herself off, creating a refuge into which could escape . . . She taught herself to participate in events without becoming part of them, how to observe without being seen. She became a voyeur, an onlooker; she developed an inner core, a private self that no one could ever know or touch."

In the summer of 1941, Janet married again, this time to Hugh Dudley Auchincloss, Jr., a wealthy New York lawyer and businessman with impeccable social credentials. Although he had been married twice before, she believed he was everything Jack Bouvier was not—pleasant, mature and stable. He was living in Washington, working for the government. Janet and the children joined him at Merrywood, his Virginia estate. His mother and benefactor was the former Emma Brewster Jennings, daughter of Oliver Jennings, a founder of Standard Oil with John D. Rockefeller.

Jackie Bouvier and her mother, Mrs. John V. Bouvier 3rd, at their Easthampton, L.I. home, August, 1933.

Jackie liked her new stepfather, but found him tedious at times. She would make fun of him behind his back. She and her sister continued to see their father frequently, and he continued to indulge them.

From her earliest days, Jackie attracted attention, as much for her intelligence as her beauty. John H. Davis, a cousin who authored a Bouvier family history, described her as a young woman who outwardly seemed to conform to social norms. But, he wrote, she possessed a "fiercely independent inner life which she shared with few people and would one day be partly responsible for her enormous success."

After two years in The Holton-Arms School in Washington, Jackie was enrolled in 1944 at Miss Porter's School in Farmington, Connecticut, a finishing school that in addition to its academic offerings emphasized good manners and the art of conversation. She was popular with her classmates and with the young men who visited from the prep schools nearby.

Jackie graduated from Miss Porter's in June 1947. She once fretted to a friend, "I'm sure no one will ever marry me, and I'll end up being a housemother at Farmington." In her yearbook entry, she said that her ambition in life was "not to be a housewife."

Miss Jacqueline Lee Bouvier made her social debut that summer at an afternoon tea dance for 300 guests at Hammersmith Farm, a handsome estate in Newport, Rhode Island, that her stepfather had recently inherited. Later Igor Cassini, in his syndicated Cholly Knickerbocker social column, gave her the ultimate accolade: "America is a country of traditions. Every four years we elect a president, every two years

our congressmen. And every year a new Queen of Debutantes is crowned . . . The Queen Deb of the year for 1947 is Jacqueline Bouvier, a regal brunette who has classic features and the daintiness of Dresden porcelain. She has poise, is soft-spoken and intelligent, everything the leading debutante should be."

Being Debutante of the Year did little to endear Jackie to her classmates that fall when she entered Vassar, the exclusive women's college in Poughkeepsie, New York. Her name appeared frequently in New York society columns. Walter Winchell wrote: "Jacqueline Bouvier's poise! What a gal! She's the beautiful daughter of Mrs. Hugh Auchincloss. Blessed with the looks of a fairy-tale princess, Jacqueline doesn't know the meaning of the word snob."

A friend, Selwa Showker, remembered something special about Jackie: "I don't think any reporter or biographer has ever succeeded in capturing Jackie's essence. There's an elusive quality about her, an inexplicable shyness. She doesn't reveal herself and was always very protective of her inner self . . . And obviously she was less protective of herself than in subsequent years when she became a public figure."

Being Deb of the Year did wonders for Jackie's social life, though, and most weekends she had dates. Her father was disappointed when she failed to make Daisy Chain, Vassar's honorary society, and blamed her weekends away from Vassar. Jackie replied that she *had* made the dean's list.

When summer came, Jackie made her first visit abroad with friends and a chaperon. The girls attended a Royal Garden Party at Buckingham Palace, where they met King George VI and Queen Elizabeth. Jackie was so impressed at meeting Winston Churchill that she went through the receiving line twice. They later visited Paris, Rome and other European cities before sailing for home.

Back at Vassar she learned of a program called Junior Year Abroad and decided she wanted to attend the Paris program run in conjunction with the Sorbonne. Her father agreed to pay for the program after she threatened to leave Vassar to become a fashion model.

Her year in France began with an intensive six-week French language program, during which she boarded with a French family and spoke only French. Away from the competitive atmosphere of Vassar and the tug-of-war of her divorced parents, she enjoyed what she later would describe as "the high point of my life, my happiest and most carefree year."

Returning home, she had a two-day reunion with

Jacqueline, 6 years old, and her sister Lee shown at the Annual Dog Show in Easthampton, Long Island, 1935, with their dog "Regent."

her father, then went to Washington to register for her senior year at George Washington University. George Washington lacked the élan and elegance of Vassar, but its saving grace in her eyes was its location—in the capital. She received a bachelor's degree in French literature in 1951.

While at George Washington, Jackie entered and won *Vogue's* Prix de Paris, a writing contest, defeating some 1,280 entrants from 225 colleges. Contestants were required to submit four technical papers on fashion, a personal profile, a plan for an entire issue of the magazine, and an essay on "People I Wish I Had Known" (her choices: Oscar Wilde, Charles Baudelaire and the ballet impresario Sergei Diaghilev). The prize was a one-year trainee position with the magazine—six months in Paris and six months in the New York office.

Her family persuaded her not to accept the prize, and Hugh Auchincloss gave her and her sister the summer in Europe. As the sisters traveled, they kept a scrapbook of Jackie's drawings and rhymes and Lee's anecdotal stories and gave it their mother when they returned. They rounded out their summer by visiting Bernard Berenson, art critic and collector at his estate near Florence. His advice to Jackie: "Marry someone who will constantly stimulate you—and you him."

Problems were waiting for Jackie when she returned. Her father wanted her to live and work with him in New York. Her mother promised her a better job in Washington. Jackie decided not to live with her father; his behavior was erratic, and he was gambling and drinking too much. When she told him of her decision, he accused her of coming to him only for money and of pandering to the Auchinclosses.

College students stroll along the deck of the "De Grasse" before sailing time. Left to right: Elizabeth Curth of Riverdale, NY., from Smith; Margaret Snyder of Gary, Indiana, from Smith; Jacqueline Bouvier of McLean, Va., from Vassar; Mary Ann Freedman of Stamford, Conn., from Smith; and Hester Williams of Jacksonville, Fla., from Smith College, will study in various schools and live with French families during their one year stay in France.

Hugh Auchincloss suggested that Jackie consider a career in journalism, and arranged an interview for her at the Washington *Times-Herald*. She was hired as a "gofer," fetching coffee and running errands for various editors, moved up to be the city room receptionist, then became the paper's Inquiring Photographer. Untrained and frightened, her work was barely acceptable. She found it difficult to come up with interesting questions, and her photographs rarely were in focus. One of her editors said, "She was just out of college and a socialite, somebody impressed with the world of journalism but unwilling to make the necessary sacrifices."

Jackie now was engaged to John G.W. Husted, Jr., a socially correct young man who worked on Wall Street. An announcement of the engagement appeared in the newspapers. The relationship was casual, apparently chaste, and Jackie soon cooled. She began dating other men, including Godfrey McHugh, an Air Force officer ten years her senior; William Walton, a former paratrooper who was a correspondent for Time Magazine; and Charles Bartlett, a journalist, who was a friend of John F. Kennedy, a handsome, ambitious Congressman from Massachusetts.

Bartlett later married Martha Buck, the daughter of a steel company magnate, and they decided Jack

and Jackie should meet. They arranged a dinner party at their Georgetown home, and had them sit next to each other. Jack and Jackie seemed to hit it off, but nothing seemed to come of it. A few months later, Martha convinced Jackie to invite Kennedy to be her escort at another dinner party at the Bartlett's home. They enjoyed themselves and began dating. They preferred quiet evenings with other Washington couples—Senator and Mrs. Albert Gore, Senator and Mrs. John Sherman Cooper, and Jack's brother and sister-in-law, Bobby and Ethel Kennedy.

One night Kennedy drove her home to Merrywood and as he left, his car broke down in her driveway. He walked back to the house, and Jackie gave him the keys to her stepfather's car. In the morning Hugh Auchincloss found his prized blue Bentley gone and an old, broken-down convertible with Massachusetts plates blocking the driveway.

Despite Jackie's reassurances, John Husted was beginning to realize the engagement was off. She invited him to Merrywood for the weekend, never said a word about their relationship, and on Sunday drove him to the airport. In the terminal she slipped the engagement ring off her finger and dropped it into his jacket pocket. "She didn't say much and neither did

Jacqueline Bouvier, with her father John Vernon Bouvier at Belmont, 1947.

I," recalled Husted. "There wasn't much you could say."

As Jackie became serious about Jack (now a Senator), she carefully weighed what was involved. She was attracted by his looks, charm, acerbic wit, ambition and the Kennedy fortune, which was estimated at $400 million. In the 1920s, Joe Kennedy established a million-dollar trust fund for each of his children, and by the early 1950s they had increased in value to more than ten times that figure. Both she and Jack were Catholic. They had similar personalities. She told friends that they were both "icebergs," keeping much of what they really felt submerged. On the other hand, he was twelve years older. He had a bad temper. He had health problems: a bad back and Addison's disease. He was allergic to animals. "Imagine me with someone allergic to horses!" she said to John Davis, author of *The Kennedys*.

"I don't think Jackie cared much about JFK's morals . . ." recalled John White, a friend from her newspaper days. "More important to her than his morality was that he was at the center of events and that he acquit himself well and give her a decent role in the drama. It's fair to say they both lived up to their ends of the bargain."

Jack introduced Jackie to his family in the summer of 1952 at the family compound at Hyannis on Cape Cod. The Kennedy girls thought that Jackie put on airs; she thought they were a bit bourgeois. Ambassador Joseph Kennedy, the family patriarch, was impressed, according to family friend Lem Billings, who quoted him as saying: "A politician has to have a wife, and a Catholic politician has to have a Catholic wife. She should have class. Jackie has more class than any girl we've ever seen around here."

Jackie arranged for Jack to meet her father over dinner in a New York restaurant. Jack Bouvier later told a friend that aside from needing a haircut, young Mr. Kennedy seemed "a decent chap—not what I expected. I thought he'd be more like his old man. At any rate, Jackie's madly in love with him." Jack Bouvier was in decline, drinking heavily and in financial trouble. Jack Kennedy liked him, though, and went out of his way to get to know his future father-in-law.

Jack was a cold suitor. There were no flowers or love letters. He proposed casually, then told Jackie they would delay the formal announcement of their engagement because a magazine was about to print a story, "Jack Kennedy—The Senate's Gay Young Bachelor." Meanwhile, Jackie attended the Coronation of Elizabeth II in London. The engagement was officially an-

Jacqueline Kennedy in 1952 working as an inquiring photographer for the Washington Times-Herald.

nounced on June 24, 1953. At an engagement party at the Hyannisport Golf Club, Jack slipped on Jackie's finger a twined square-cut emerald and diamond.

Jacqueline Lee Bouvier and John Fitzgerald Kennedy were joined in marriage before 750 invited guests on September 12, 1953, at St. Mary's Roman Catholic Church in Newport, Rhode Island. The Archbishop of Boston, Richard Cushing, conducted the Nuptial high mass assisted by four priests. Bobby Kennedy was best man, Lee was matron of honor. As they left the church, some 3,000 spectators tried to get a glimpse of the 36-year-old groom and his 24-year-old bride.

Jack Bouvier had looked forward to giving his daughter away, but was hurt when he arrived in Newport to learn that he was not welcome at any of the pre-wedding parties. One the morning of the wedding, he began drinking. By the time the wedding party was preparing to leave for the church, his speech was slurred and he could barely walk a straight line. Janet was furious. She arranged for Hugh Auchincloss to substitute, and sent word to her ex-husband that if he appeared at the church he would be forcibly ejected.

The reception at Hammersmith Farm, the Auchincloss estate, was attended by more than 1,300 guests, a combination of Irish politicians and the Republican establishment friends of Hugh and Janet Auchincloss. Huge tents had been set up on the back lawn, the sun shown, the guests danced to Meyer Davis and *Life* photographers blazed away.

The newlyweds spent their wedding night in the honeymoon suite at the Waldorf-Astoria in New York,

9

then flew to Acapulco for their honeymoon. They stayed at the villa of Don Miguel Aleman, President of Mexico and an old friend of Joe Kennedy. On their way home, they stopped in San Francisco and stayed with Jack's friends, Paul and Anita Fay. In his book, *The Pleasure of His Company*, Paul noted that his friend was still flirting shamelessly with every attractive female who came his way. Jack described himself to Paul as "both too old and too young for marriage."

Jacqueline Bouvier's debutante portrait.

Chapter 2

From the beginning, marriage to Jack Kennedy was not easy. Jackie had hoped for a life of comfort and perfection in a world of their own. Now she faced a vast, unruly public life. Jack would take her to parties and leave her while he worked the room, building his political contacts.

For most of their first year of married life, they lived with their parents, dividing their time between Merrywood in Virginia and the Kennedy compound on Cape Cod. They spent Christmas of 1953 with his parents in Palm Beach. Jackie enjoyed the company of Joe Kennedy, whose womanizing didn't bother her. According to Lem Billings, a family friend: "[Joe] enjoyed talking about his female conquests. For hours he would tell Jackie about Gloria Swanson, Marion Davies and countless others, past and present. He and Jackie shared personal feelings and private jokes.

"When Jackie and Jack had problems, she would unburden herself to Joe. He admired her strength, the fact that she always maintained her own identity. She was the one person who could stand up to the old man and get away with it." Jackie and her father-in-law formed an alliance: "he paid her bills and she discreetly put up with his son's philandering."

In the spring of 1954, the Kennedys rented a small 19th-century townhouse in the Georgetown section of Washington, but when the six-month lease was up they moved to a hotel. "During our first year of marriage, we were gypsies living in and out of a suitcase," Jackie told an interviewer. "That first year I longed for a home of our own. I hoped it would give our lives some roots, some stability. My ideal at that time was a normal life with my husband coming home from work every day at five. I wanted him to spend weekends with me and the children we would have."

Jackie worked hard at becoming a good hostess. She took cooking lessons and learned about wine. She helped Jack become a more effective public speaker. She took charge of his wardrobe and packed his bag when he went on trips. She was in the Senate gallery when Jack gave important speeches, attended political rallies and receptions, cocktail parties and luncheons, and joined the Senate Red Cross committee and a Senate wives cultural group. She became pregnant but miscarried.

In the fall of 1955, Jack and Jackie began putting down roots. They acquired one of the homes in the Kennedy compound, and they purchased Hickory Hill, a white brick Georgian mansion in Virginia, two miles from Merrywood. The property had stables for Jackie's horses and a swimming pool for Jack to exercise his back which had been operated on the year before. Jackie redecorated the house, paying particular attention to the nursery.

A year later, Jackie was again pregnant and Jack was planning for the 1956 Democratic Convention in Chicago where he was a dark-horse candidate to be Adlai Stevenson's running mate. After Stevenson was nominated on the first ballot, he decided to let the convention select his running mate. The Kennedy team swung into action. Jack convinced Connecticut Governor Abe Ribcoff to nominate him and George Smathers to second the nomination. When it was all over, Jack had lost to Estes Kefauver, but had come closer than anyone thought he would.

On the spur of the moment, Jack decided to fly to France the next day with Smathers to visit Joe Kennedy who was vacationing on the Riviera. Jackie pleaded with him to stay and accompany her to Newport. She hated flying, particularly now that she was pregnant. When he wouldn't change his mind, she decided to join her mother and stepfather at Hammersmith Farm

A week after her arrival in Rhode Island, Jackie suffered severe cramps and began to hemorrhage. She was rushed to the hospital and underwent an emergency Cesarean. The fetus, that of a girl, was stillborn. Bobby Kennedy flew to her side. Jack was cruising on a yacht; three days passed before he learned about Jackie's miscarriage. Told that Jackie was all right, he decided to continue his vacation, but George Smathers and his father changed his mind. "If you want to run for president, you'd better get your ass back to your wife's bedside or else every wife in the country will be against you," Smathers recalled saying. "'Why the hell should I go now?' he asked. I told him I was going to get him back there even if I had to carry him. Joe Kennedy agreed, so we went back together.'"

Jackie was still in the hospital when the family held a memorial service for the little girl who did not live long enough to be christened. After a few days with his wife, Jack was off to campaign for the Stevenson-Kefauver ticket, making 140 public appearances in

Hyannisport, June 27, 1953. Jack and Jackie as an engaged couple.

twenty-six states.

Eisenhower was reelected by a landslide, and Jack decided it was just as well that he hadn't been on the ticket. Stevenson's defeat might have been blamed on his Catholicism, which would have ruled out another opportunity for high office. Now he was in control of his political destiny. He was forty years old, nationally known as the handsome young senator who delivered the Stevenson nominating speech at the convention, and was already being mentioned as a possible Presidential contender.

In 1957 he was awarded the Pulitzer Prize for his book *Profiles in Courage*. A scandal nearly erupted over how much of the book Jack actually wrote. His father hushed that up, bought up thousands of copies to put the book on the best-seller list, and had his friend, the distinguished New York *Times* columnist Arthur Krock,

lobby the members of the Pulitzer board in behalf of Jack's book. Joe told his son, "You would be surprised how a book that really makes the grade with high-class people stands you in good stead for years to come."

The Washington rumor mill reported that the Kennedys were rarely seen together and were having marital problems. Published reports had the marriage already over. *Time* magazine said Jackie had threatened divorce and Joe Kennedy had made a million-dollar deal with her to stay with his son. It wasn't true, but Joe did impress on her the importance of staying together to make things work. What Jack needed most to settle him down, he said, was a child.

Jackie was determined to have a baby. The nursery at Hickory Hill reminded Jackie of her miscarriages, so Jack bought a house on N Street in Georgetown and gave Jackie carte blanche in decorating it. She retained the famed New York decorator Sister Parish but made all the decisions herself. "She loved surrounding herself with beautiful objects," recalled Elisabeth Draper, who helped her decorate Hickory Hill, "[but she] wanted to make their new home as much his as hers."

While she was involved in the new house, Jackie's father died of liver cancer. She flew to New York to be at his side, but arrived an hour too late. His last word had been "Jackie." She was deeply upset but pulled herself together and saw to the funeral arrangements. She wrote his obituary and to accompany it recovered a photograph from one of her father's women friends. She selected St. Patrick's Cathedral for the funeral, and ordered the closed coffin covered with a thick blanket of yellow daisies and white bachelor's buttons. She neither cried nor showed emotion at the service or at the burial at the Bouvier family plot in East Hampton.

On November 27, 1957, four months after the death of her father, Jacqueline Kennedy gave birth at New York's Lying-In Hospital to a healthy baby girl. Delivered by cesarean section, Caroline Bouvier Kennedy weighed 7 pounds, 2 ounces. The proud father said she looked "as robust as a sumo wrestler." Three weeks later she was christened at St. Patrick's Cathedral, wearing the same robe Jackie had worn at her own christening. Everyone was pleased. The marriage improved.

The birth of Caroline and moving into their new Georgetown home gave Jackie confidence. She now felt comfortable, insulated from the Kennedy clan and her own domineering mother. She realized that the Kennedys were public figures who fed on publicity, and she would have to make accommodations to them. She told an interviewer, "I wouldn't say that being married to a very busy politician is the easiest life to adjust to.

Jack and Jackie, the newlyweds cut their wedding cake.

The wedding party.

But you think about it and figure out the best way to do things—to keep the house running smoothly, to spend as much time as you can with your husband and your children—and eventually you find your self well adjusted."

Jackie played an active role in Jack's Senatorial reelection campaign. Larry O'Brien, who directed the campaign, recalled that Jackie was, "a refreshing change from the usual candidate's wife because she did not bother to put on a phony show of enthusiasm about everything she saw and every local politician whom she met. The crowds sensed that and it impressed them. When Jackie traveled with the Kennedy bandwagon, the crowds were twice as big."

A Democratic district leader, William DeMarco, recalled Jackie's appearance at the Michelangelo School in Boston's Italian North End: "The gracious lady stood up before the big crowd, and the Italian people, the elderly people who were there, didn't know who she was. But when she opened her mouth and introduced herself in Italian, fluent Italian may I say, as the wife of Senator Kennedy, all pandemonium broke loose. All the people went over and started to kiss her, and the old women spoke to her as if she was a native of the North End. And I think her talk is actually what cemented the relationship between Senator Kennedy and the Italian-Americans of the district. They figured that not only was he the representative of the district, he was one of them."

"Politics is in my blood," she said, "the most exciting life imaginable." Sometimes, however, she simply refused to go campaigning and instead would go for long walks. On one occasion, as Jack was shaking hands with constituents, a reporter spotted her in the back of a campaign car, looking bored and flipping the pages of a fashion magazine.

Mary Tierney, who covered the 1958 campaign, recalled, "Jackie didn't go for full-fledged interviews unless she could control them. I thought she was a dummy, to be honest about it. I didn't think she was capable of talking about too much of anything, no less political affairs. She had that breathless approach and just didn't seem too interested. She hated campaigning . . . She didn't have that feeling for campaigning that he did."

National campaigning was more endurable for Jackie than the local Massachusetts outings. She accompanied Jack to a fund-raiser in Los Angeles in the spring of 1958. "Her glamour and her unconventional beauty attracted attention and enticed the news media, for whom the couple had become a symbol of youth and vitality—a new symbol for a New Age," said a party official. "They looked more like movie stars."

Jackie told Larry O'Brien that she learned more about human nature during her first year on the campaign trail than she had from all her previous experiences combined. "She joined us on the traditional elec-

Wedding portrait of Jacqueline Lee Bouvier. She and John Fitzgerald Kennedy were married on Saturday, September 12, 1953 in Newport, Rhode Island's St. Mary's Church. Archbishop Richard J. Cushing officiated at the wedding and nuptial mass.

tion-eve tour of the Boston wards, which in those days culminated at the G and G Delicatessen on Blue Hill Avenue in Dorchester," he said. "Jack, Bob and Ted climbed atop a table and sang 'Heart of My Heart'—off-key but exuberantly."

When the returns were in, Jack Kennedy had defeated Vincent Celeste, a Boston lawyer, by a record 874,000 votes, a three-to-one ratio. The national media covered his sweeping victory. He now turned his attention to 1960.

Joe Kennedy's dream was to have a son in the White House, and he took charge of Jack's presidential campaign from the very beginning. "It became Joe's run for the roses as much as Jack's," said George Smathers. "Joe Kennedy masterminded the whole campaign, just as he had masterminded Jack's initial entry into politics after Joe Jr.'s death. 'We're going to sell Jack like cornflakes,' he boasted. He'd begun lining up political bosses as early as 1957, starting with Mayor Richard Daley of Chicago . . . He understood that what you did was to merchandise a concept and he had enough experience in Hollywood and the motion picture business to grope around in that whole area, which has now become common practice.

"The 1960 campaign was Joe's show entirely, yet he managed to organize it from behind the scenes. Because of his past record, he was forced to stay out of the limelight. But he called the shots, and you could sense his influence and imprint on many of Jack's ideas."

Until she became pregnant again, Jackie joined Jack on many of his early campaign outings. She spoke Spanish in New York City, French in Eau Clair, Italian in Syracuse, even a smattering of Polish in Milwaukee. She taped interviews and campaign messages in foreign languages for radio and television. She gave luncheons at her home in Georgetown. She spoke to shoppers at supermarkets. She and Jack crisscrossed the country aboard the *Caroline*, a twin-engine Corvair purchased by Joe Kennedy at a cost of $350,000.

"There were two phases to the campaign," Larry O'Brien remembered. "First we had to win the Democratic nomination; then we had to beat Richard Nixon. The first part came easier to Jackie because she wasn't pregnant. And by then she had become a seasoned traveler, learning to subsist on 'fast foods' and to live on the road with only three dresses—one for morning, one for afternoon, one for evening—and one hat for church. Her jewelry consisted of a string of pearls. She also took a traveling iron and a sewing kit. By this point she had learned how to hustle a crowd, force herself onto a plat-

The youthful parents with their two-year-old daughter, Caroline.

form in front of 5,000 screaming strangers, shake 10,000 hands without collapsing of fatigue."

Jackie's first major test came in March 1960, when Jack, neck-and-neck with Hubert Humphrey in the Wisconsin primary, had to return to Washington for a critical vote in the Senate. "I'll carry on for you," said Jackie. Then, accompanied by Ted Kennedy, she traveled from town to town, giving short speeches at every stop. She told seventy-five people at a luncheon in Marshfield: "We've been working so hard in Wisconsin, and I know that if you do see fit to support my husband you will find you haven't misplaced your trust. In recent years he has served on the Senate Labor and Public Welfare Committee and in that capacity has done as much for workers in this country as any U.S. Senator. He will continue to do everything in his power if elected President."

Kennedy defeated Humphrey in Wisconsin by 106,000 votes. Some thought Jackie made the difference. She thought Jack won because of his valor under fire. The media attributed it to the large number of Catholic votes in Wisconsin.

The next primary was the heavily Protestant West Virginia. Kennedy's surprise victory there was a major turning point in his campaign. "At that moment we

President-elect Kennedy looks on as Jacqueline holds John F. Kennedy, Jr., after the baby was christened in the Georgetown Hospital chapel.

realized he could win it all," recalled Charles Peters, a Kennedy organizer in West Virginia. "If he'd lost, we knew he could lose it all. It was clear there was a great deal riding on it. Never before had so much ridden on something so small as a primary in a state like West Virginia." Jack and Jackie were in Washington on election night. When Bobby Kennedy phoned with news of the victory, they immediately flew to Kanawha, West Virginia, to personally thank their supporters. As he stepped from the Caroline, Kennedy told reporters: "I

think we have now buried the religious issue once and for all."

Once at the West Virginia victory celebration, however, Jack ignored Jackie. "She seemed miserable at being left out of things," recalled Ben Bradlee. "And this night she and Tony [Bradlee's wife] stood on a stairway, totally ignored, as JFK made his victory statement on television. Later when Kennedy was enjoying his greatest moment of triumph to date, Jackie quietly disappeared and went out to the car and sat by herself until he was ready to fly back to Washington."

When Kennedy arrived at the Democratic convention in Los Angeles in July, he had 761 delegate votes and victory was assured. Just before he walked into the convention hall to accept the nomination, he called Jackie in Hyannisport. "It's a good thing you didn't come out here," he said. "There's too much pandemonium. You can watch me on TV in a few minutes. I'll call you later to see how you liked it."

At the urging of his father, Kennedy chose Senator Lyndon Johnson of Texas as his running mate to the dismay of liberals, campaign aides, labor leaders, civil rights activists and brother Bobby, his campaign manager.

A victory celebration was held that night at Pat and Peter Lawford's California house. The guests, including Jack, Bobby, Pierre Salinger and Angie Dickinson, got drunk and went skinny-dipping in the pool. The party became so noisy that neighbors called the police, who nearly took the half-naked celebrants to the station before recognizing Jack.

Meeting with reporters that day, Jackie said, "I suppose I won't be able to play much part in the campaign but I'll do what I can. I feel I should be with Jack when he's engaged in such a struggle and if it weren't for the baby, I'd campaign even more vigorously than Mrs. Nixon."

Jackie had problems dealing with the press. When asked where she thought the Democratic convention should be held, she replied, "Acapulco." When Kennedy's Catholicism became an issue, she told a reporter, "I think it's so unfair of people to be against Jack because he's a Catholic. He's such a poor Catholic. Now, if it were Bobby, I could understand it." She told a reporter, "A newspaper reported Sunday that I spent $30,000 buying Paris clothes and that women hate me for it. I couldn't possibly spend that much unless I wore sable underwear." When Jack read the story he exploded: "Good Christ! That's the last interview that goddamned woman will give until after the election!"

Jackie frequently said she was nervous and was doubtful about the outcome. This irritated Jack, who was confident he would win. Four months before the election, he told her to start looking for a White House social secretary and someone to handle press relations.

On the morning of election day, Jack and Jackie flew to Boston to vote, then returned to Hyannisport to watch the returns on television.

After dinner, Jack and Jackie joined the rest of the

Senator Kennedy and his wife, Jacqueline get down to an evening of studying after dinner.

Sloan Simpson, Mrs. John F. Kennedy, and stage star Celeste Holm, pose prettily at the "Bal de la Soie" Annual April in Paris Ball at the Waldorf-Astoria.

Senator and Mrs. John F. Kennedy enjoy a final sail in the 32 ft. Wianno Senior sailboat before his return to the Senate floor.

clan at Bobby's house to tabulate the votes. At 3 a.m., when the Nixons appeared on television, Jackie turned to her husband and said, "Oh, Bunny. You're the President now." "No, not yet," he replied. Then he walked off by himself to go to bed.

Kennedy won by the narrow margin of 118,550 votes. A television newsman commented that only 24,000 more votes in five states would have elected Nixon. "Well, what the hell," snorted Joe Kennedy. "Did you expect me to pay for a landslide?"

On the morning of the victory, while the Kennedys played touch football, Jackie walked to the beach to be alone. Passing groups of photographers who called out their good wishes, she walked by, turning her head so they wouldn't see her tears. She was frightened and overwhelmed by the prospect of being First Lady.

Chapter 3

Returning to Washington after the election, Jackie was confused, unhappy and eight months pregnant. She knew that as First Lady her every public action would invite comment. She was overrun by campaign aides, new appointees, Senate staffers, Secret Service agents, secretaries and platoons of reporters and television newsmen. "I feel as though I have just turned into a piece of public property," she said. "It's really frightening to lose your anonymity at thirty-one."

Crowds of tourists collected in front of the Kennedys' Georgetown house hoping to get a glimpse of the couple. Having Jack "underfoot all the time," she said, conducting business at home, jumping up to wave from the window at strangers, was a constant irritation. To Jack, who thrived on the confusion, she said, "I can't stand this chaos, Jack. It's driving me crazy." He snapped, "Oh, for God's sake, Jackie. All you have to worry about right now is your inaugural ball gown. Let Tish [Baldridge] do the rest."

In November, Kennedy went to spend a week at Lyndon Johnson's Texas ranch, then to Palm Beach to relax with his parents. He returned to have Thanksgiving dinner with Jackie and Caroline, but insisted on returning to Florida that evening. "Why can't you stay here until I have the baby and then we can go down together?" Jackie asked, but Jack refused to change his plans.

An hour after her husband left, Jackie was resting in her bedroom when she suddenly called for Caroline's nurse. The nurse quickly realized that the baby was arriving four weeks early. She phoned the doctor and Jackie was rushed to Georgetown University Hospital, where she underwent an emergency Cesarean operation.

Kennedy was startled when the news was radioed to him on his private plane. "I'm never there when she needs me," he said. Landing at Palm Beach, he boarded the press plane to return to Washington. At 1:17 a.m. the plane's radio brought news of the birth of John Fitzgerald Kennedy, Jr. The reporters aboard applauded wildly.

The baby spent his first six days in an incubator. The day of the christening, Kennedy arrived at the hospital to push Jackie in a wheelchair to the chapel. Seeing a group of reporters and photographers at the end of the hall, he slowed down. "Oh, God. Don't stop,

Joseph P. Kennedy, his wife, Rose, with their son, John, and his wife, Jacqueline, on November 9th 1960, shortly after receiving official word that John had been elected President.

Jack," she pleaded. "Just keep going." But aware that this was the first baby ever born to a President-elect and his wife, Kennedy allowed the photographers to take a few pictures.

Jackie convalesced at the Kennedy home in Palm Beach, but it was as frenzied as her Georgetown house. "It was so crowded," she complained, "that I could be in the bathroom, in the tub, and then find that Pierre Salinger was holding a press conference in my bedroom." She refused to join the rest of the clan for meals, preferring to eat in her room.

While in Palm Beach, seamstresses from Bergdorf Goodman arrived to fit the white silk crepe gown Jackie had designed for the Inaugural Ball. To Jackie the ball was not a party, it was a political pay-off. But as it would be televised, she was determined to be seen as a regal First Lady. Her gown was stunning: a silver-threaded bodice under a sheer white chiffon over-blouse. It was deceptively simple and exquisitely detailed. Owning

Senator Kennedy and wife with Senator Johnson and his wife.

no spectacular jewelry herself, Jackie had arranged to borrow from Tiffany a diamond pin and pendant diamond earrings to complete the ensemble. Jack found out about the loan and forbade it. But Jackie told Tish Baldrige to go ahead, warning Tiffany that if the story was leaked to the press she would do no more business with them.

Jack Kennedy was eager to leave Palm Beach and return to Washington. He accepted every Inaugural party invitation with enthusiasm. Although he didn't enjoy classical music, he looked forward to the Inaugural Concert at Constitutional Hall. Five balls were being held throughout the city, and he was determined to dance at each of them. He would sit four hours to see the Inaugural parade. He was excited about the Hollywood celebrities who would entertain at the fundraising gala being staged by Peter Lawford and Frank Sinatra. He was proud that Robert Frost would recite one of his poems at the swearing-in ceremony, and that Marian Anderson would sing "The Star-Spangled Banner." He was as excited as a small boy at Christmas.

Jackie, though, dreaded the Inaugural festivities. To her they involved pushing crowds, sweaty handshakes, blinding lights. She insisted that Pierre Salinger issue a statement saying, "On the advice of her doctors, Mrs. Kennedy will restrict her participation to the main inaugural ceremonies and festivities."

She refused to attend the reception for distinguished women at the National Gallery because she would be in a receiving line to greet 4,500 guests. Nor would she go the reception for Vice President and Mrs. Johnson, whom she referred to as "Colonel Cornpone

and his little pork chop." She also vetoed the Young Democrats' dance, the Governors' reception, and a dinner-dance given by Jean Kennedy Smith and her husband. The new President went to most of these events alone.

On Inauguration Day, Kennedy attended mass at Holy Trinity Church and returned home to rehearse his speech. While Jackie ate breakfast, her ball gown was taken to the White House for her to wear that evening. Tish Baldrige was already at the White House supervising the movers and preparing for the afternoon reception. President Eisenhower had invited the Kennedys to stop by for coffee before proceeding to the Capitol. Jack pleaded with Jackie to be ready on time. While dressing, Kennedy realized he couldn't fasten his collar because of the weight he had gained since the election. He sent his chauffeur to get one from his father who was staying nearby.

When the limousine arrived, Kennedy was waiting, resplendent in his cutaway coat, light pearl waistjacket, gray striped trousers and top hat. Jackie was still putting on her make-up. "For God's sake, Jackie, let's

Enjoying their tumultuous reception, Sen. Kennedy and wife Jacqueline ride through the "Canyon of Heroes" in a ticker tape parade, October 19, 1960. The Democratic Presidential nominee arrived to campaign for New York's important 45 electoral votes.

Swearing in of President-Elect Kennedy.

go," he pleaded. Finally she appeared, elegant in a beige wool suit with a sable collar, a matching sable muff, and a beige pillbox hat. She would be the only woman on the President's platform not wrapped in mink.

On the way from the White House to the Capitol, the atmosphere between the Eisenhowers and the Kennedys was strained. Mamie pointed to Eisenhower and said, "Doesn't Ike look like Paddy the Irishman in his top hat?" Neither Jack nor Jackie said a word.

At noon on January 20, 1960, Dwight David Eisenhower, at seventy the oldest man to have served

as President, was succeeded by John Fitzgerald Kennedy, at forty-three the youngest man ever to be elected to the office. He also would be the first Roman Catholic President and the first President to be born in the 20th century.

Unlike earlier Presidents, Kennedy did not kiss his wife after the ceremony. He bounded off the platform as if he had forgotten she was there. In the rotunda of the Capitol, when they met for the first time as President and First Lady, she tried to show her love but was unable to express herself. "I was so proud of Jack," she

President Kennedy fixes his wife's wind-blown coiffure as they leave Blair House for the White House, May 3, 1961. They had just met President and Mrs. Bourguiba of Tunisia, at the airport and had taken part in an open-air parade through the streets of Washington.

recalled. "There was so much I wanted to say. But I could scarcely embrace him in front of all those people, so I remember I just put my hand on his cheek and said, 'Jack, you were so wonderful!' And he was smiling in the most touching and most vulnerable way. He looked so happy."

In the afternoon, the temperature was barely above freezing as floats, bands, and units from the armed forces paraded up Pennsylvania Avenue and passed in review before the new President. He was determined to see it all, but after an hour Jackie was bored. She pleaded fatigue and went back to the White House to rest.

While she was getting dressed for the evening, Jack went to a dinner party for a group of friends who had chartered a plane and campaigned in various states for him. One of the guests recalled, "Jack probably had

more fun without her there because he could really relax and not worry about her having a good time. After all, it was a party for the people who had worked for him—not her."

The President returned to the White House well after nine to pick up his wife. Vice President and Mrs. Johnson had been waiting for her to come down for about twenty minutes. When Jackie heard Jack come in, she came downstairs in a sheath of white chiffon, her borrowed diamonds and a billowing floor-length white silk cape. "Darling, I've never seen you look so lovely. Your dress is beautiful."

They began to make the rounds of the Inaugural balls. They would enter to the strains of "Hail to the Chief" and the crowd would applaud. From Jackie's expression it was clear that she enjoyed the attention but not the clamor. At the second ball, the President left Jackie to look in on a private party hosted by Frank Sinatra for the celebrities who had performed the night before. By the time he came back, Jackie was annoyed. She said no one was dancing and the balls lacked dignity. "Just a bunch of people milling around like mesmerized cattle," she said. The President ignored her and started hopping from one box to another, greeting friends. She had had enough festivities by the time they reached the third ball. "I just crumpled," she recalled.

"All my strength was finally gone, so I went home and Jack went on to the others."

Around two in the morning, the President went to the Georgetown home of Joseph Alsop, the political columnist, to have a nightcap with a small party of friends. The next day, when the press asked about the President's late visit, Alsop said discretely, "Well, the President was hungry, and so I fed him terrapin."

Jackie at July14, 1960 press conference.

President and Mrs. John F. Kennedy leave the White House, Jan. 20, 1961 to attend a series of inaugural balls. The First Lady's dress was designed by Oleg Cassini.

Lady Bird Johnson, wife of the Vice President, escorts Jackie into the Supreme Court Chamber where she was the honor guest at a luncheon of the Senate wives.

Chapter 4

Jackie was determined to carve out a role of her own in the Kennedy presidency. During the early months, though, her greatest impact was on style. She revolutionized dress for a female public figure. She loved slacks and shorts and riding habits. She did not overdress—ever. She dispensed with the klutzy handbags, the fussy hats, the grim shoes, the clashing colors and the unphotogenic prints. Halston made her the famous pillbox hat. Because Kennedy insisted she wear only American fashions in the White House, she appointed Oleg Cassini as the official designer, the first time in history a First Lady had made such a designation. At Jackie's insistence, Cassini made copies of current French couture, while she encouraged people to believe she bought American. Because her excellent taste was always restrained, it was nearly impossible to tell the difference.

She found her mission in the restoration of the White House. "I think the White House should show the wonderful heritage that this country has," she explained. She decided "to throw out all the crap," as she referred to the Grand Rapids reproduction furniture. She banished "Pullman-car ashtrays," the "seasick green curtains" and all the other "eyesore ornamentation." She called the ground floor hall "a dentist's office bomb shelter," and the East Room "a roller-skating rink." "It looks like a house where nothing has taken place. There is no trace of the past."

The President initially opposed the idea of her tearing through the mansion, throwing out furniture and rearranging everything, but Jackie persuaded him that the White House had to be restored to stand as the finest American home in the country. She asked Sister Parrish, the New York decorator, to redo the private living quarters. "Let's have lots of chintz and gay up this old dump," she commanded.

Jackie and her committees hired curators, drafted legislation, recruited scholars and solicited contributions. She convinced private donors to part with their historic furniture and art museums to lend her more than 150 paintings. Within a year she had transformed the White House into a national monument with antiques and heirlooms worth more than $10 million.

Despite her obsession with her personal privacy, Jackie wanted as much publicity as possible on her restoration project. She realized that press coverage would encourage private gifts for the restoration and build public interest in the White House. She made appearances, posed for pictures, wrote letters, signed autographs. When CBS contacted her about the possibility of a televised tour of the restored White House, she quickly accepted. Without the help of a script, the First Lady strolled through the White House rooms, describing gifts and mentioning the names of the donors in her whispery voice. More than forty-six million people watched the program. The Chicago *Daily News* called it "television at its best."

The social skills Jackie acquired at East Hampton and Farmington and Vassar were much in evidence in the White House. Her parties were nothing short of spectacular. "I think she cast a particular spell over the White House that has not been equaled," recalled Benjamin C. Bradlee, former executive editor of *The Washington Post*. "She was young. My God, she was young. She had great taste, a sense of culture, an understanding of art. She brought people like André Malraux to the White House who never would have gone there. As personalities, they really transformed the city."

Her sense of humor appealed to Tish Baldrige, Jackie's chief of staff and special secretary in the White House, who had preceded her by two years at Farmington and Vassar. "She had such a wit. She would have been terrible if she hadn't been so funny. She imitated people, heads of state, after everyone had left a White House dinner. Their accents, the way they talked. She was a cutup."

The President encouraged Caroline to talk to reporters and allowed photographers into the Oval Office specifically to take her picture. Jackie hated to see her children used for publicity purposes. Every time she saw a photograph of them which she had not authorized, she would complain to Press Secretary Pierre Salinger. He would meekly explain that the picture was taken at the request of the President. "I don't give a damn," Jackie replied. "He has no right to countermand my order regarding the children."

Jackie's battles with the press were never-ending. She ordered high rhododendron bushes planted to shield Caroline's playground from view. She instructed the Secret Service to confiscate film from photographers who took pictures without her permission. The children's pets also were out-of-bounds. After reading

Mrs. Kennedy visits with Shrimati Indra Gandhi in New Delhi, India, March 14, 1962.

an innocuous account of Charlie, the Kennedys' Welsh terrier, she railed at the kennel-keeper: "Don't you ever give another thing to those damn nosy reporters." A photographer followed Jackie to Virginia and took a picture of her being thrown from her horse. She called the White House and demanded that the photographer be banned from ever using the picture on the grounds that it was an invasion of privacy. "I'm sorry, Jackie," an amused Kennedy replied, "but when the First Lady falls on her ass, that's news."

Jackie made it clear that she would not perform the traditional role of the First Lady. "Why the hell should I traipse around to hospitals playing Lady Bountiful when I have so much to do here to make this house livable? I'll just send them some fruits and nuts and flowers." She refused to attend political events. She avoided ceremonial duties and anything she considered "boring and a useless waste of my time." Despite Kennedy's commitment to civil rights, she refused to attend a luncheon of the National Council of Negro Women. Nor did she attend the Congressional wives' prayer breakfast.

"Kennedy's only complaint about Jackie in all the years I ever knew him was that she spent too much money," said Senator George Smathers. "And I always laughed when he'd start bitching about it because if there was any guy who had no regard for money it was Jack Kennedy."

The Kennedy European trip in 1961 was a turning point in their relationship. Kennedy began to realize that he had underestimated Jackie's public impact. She was a tremendous success in France. Of course, she was of French descent, and proud of it. She had lived in Paris for a year while studying at the Sorbonne and had fallen in love with the city. Now the city fell in love with her.

Parisians lined the streets for hours waiting for her arrival. As the motorcade pulled into view, they would scream: "Jacquiii! Jacquiii! Jacquiii!" Kennedy was overwhelmed by the extraordinary impression his wife was making. At a press conference, he told reporters: "I do not think it altogether inappropriate to introduce myself to this audience. I am the man who accompanied Jacqueline Kennedy to Paris, and I have enjoyed it."

Jackie even charmed Charles de Gaulle, the President of France, who said "Ah, the gracious Mrs. Kennedy," when they met. De Gaulle later told Kennedy, "Your wife knows more French history than any French woman." "The First Lady is bursting with youth and beauty," said *Le Figaro*.

Some say that after the visit to Paris, the glory of France became Jackie's standard of excellence. She wanted all state visitors to leave the White House as impressed as she had been with the Palace of Versailles.

As the President-elect follows, Mrs. Kennedy leaves her box after attending the Inaugural Gala January 19, 1960. The two watched as a parade of show-business people put on a special show to help pay off Kennedy's campaign debts.

Her table now was set with gold flatware dating back to James Monroe. Stodgy potted palms were replaced with topiary trees reminiscent of the Tuileries Gardens. For state dinners, she insisted on serving French wine.

America's leading musicians and actors were invited to perform at the White House. Metropolitan Opera stars Roberta Peters and Jerome Hines sang for President Manuel Prado of Peru. Eugene List gave a piano recital for Harry Truman. President Ferik Ibrahim Abboud of Sudan was impressed by a performance by the American Shakespeare Festival of Stratford, Connecticut. Jackie brought Pablo Casals out of exile to perform at the state dinner in honor of Puerto Rican Governor Luis Munoz.

Jackie's most ambitious and dramatic state dinner was a candlelight dinner on the lawn of Mount Vernon, George Washington's plantation overlooking the Potomac. The logistics were staggering. Fleets of government yachts were commandeered to transport the guests down the river from Washington. Army trucks carried the White House china, silver and gold ballroom chairs. The National Park Service set up portable kitchens for the White House chef's gourmet dinner. A bandstand was built for the National Symphony Orchestra. A tent pavilion was decorated with garlands of greenery. Army bands played before dinner and Marines in dress uniforms lined the road from the Mount Vernon dock to the mansion. The 'Strolling Strings' of the Air Force lilted while mint juleps were served in silver cups. The evening was a triumph. The next day Jackie flew to Hyannisport for the summer. "I've just got to relax," she told the President. "This party took every ounce of energy I had."

Mrs. Jacqueline Kennedy distributes gifts and chats with children at the National Institute for the Protection of Children, during a visit to Mexico City.

President and Mrs. Kennedy arrived in Palm Beach May 11, 1961 where they will spend a long week-end. The President and First Lady are shown as they arrived at the Palm Beach airport.

Jackie, John, and Caroline, November 11, 1961.

Chapter 5

In April 1961, Kennedy committed his biggest blunder as President—the Bay of Pigs, a disastrous attempt to land 1,200 exile troops in Cuba to overthrow Castro. In an attempt to help Jack relax, she invited Paul and Anita Fay and Bobby and Ethel Kennedy to a small dinner party. Jackie tried to keep the conversation light, but Bobby kept bringing up Cuba and the eighty-seven men who lost their lives and the survivors who were being held for ransom. "I'll never again accept the recommendations of the Joint Chiefs of Staff without first challenging them," vowed the President, complaining bitterly about the faulty information he was given. As the evening wore on, the President became more and more serious. After dinner, Jackie told Paul Fay: "You know, I had hoped we were going to have a pleasant dinner instead of having Jack go through another one of those sessions on the Bay of Pigs."

During the missile crisis of October 1962, Jackie agonized with her husband. The night the President appeared on television to break the news of the Soviet missile buildup taking place in Cuba, she held a small black-tie party for him at the White House, trying once again to relieve the tension. As the country risked war with the Soviet Union, she led her guests to the piano. People fidgeted as she tried to dispel the unspoken feeling that this was hardly the appropriate time for singing. Recalled one guest: "She tried desperately to jolly the party along so that, first and foremost, the President could enjoy a brief respite from the crisis."

"We never talked of serious things," Jackie said. "I guess because Jack always told me the one thing a busy man doesn't want to talk about at the end of the day is whether the Geneva Convention will be successful or what settlement could be made in Kashmir or anything like that. He didn't tell me those things. He wanted me as a wife, and seldom brought home his working problems—except, once in a while, the serious ones."

Jackie was concerned when Joe Kennedy, her seventy-three-old father-in-law, suffered a stroke, which would leave him paralyzed for the rest of his life. Although he was confined to a wheelchair and was unable to speak, except in unintelligible grunts, she insisted that he be included in private White House dinner parties. She would tease him affectionately and talk to him fondly about many things. She liked to remind him how he had urged his son to marry her. From the

President and Mrs. Kennedy pose before the White House Christmas tree in the Blue Room prior to a party they gave to the White House staff. The tree's usual decorations and tinsel have been replaced with ginger bread cookies, candy and toys.

beginning, Joe Kennedy had been her one good friend within the family. Jackie was devoted to him for the rest of her life.

Jack Kennedy never accepted women as equals, and tended to treat his wife as a child. Occasionally her silliness would irritate him. Once, while he was waiting to be photographed, she took a floral wreath and hung it around his neck like a racehorse. "Damn it, Jackie, take this thing off me, and don't act so stupid. I can't be photographed this way, for Christ's sake." A bit giggly on champagne, Jackie responded by making funny faces at him.

"Jack thoroughly enjoyed being President, and unlike Jackie, who had such a hard time adjusting, never once got bored in the White House," recalled a friend. "When she finished the restoration project and started getting restless, he babied her a little bit, encouraging her to take that trip to India and Pakistan

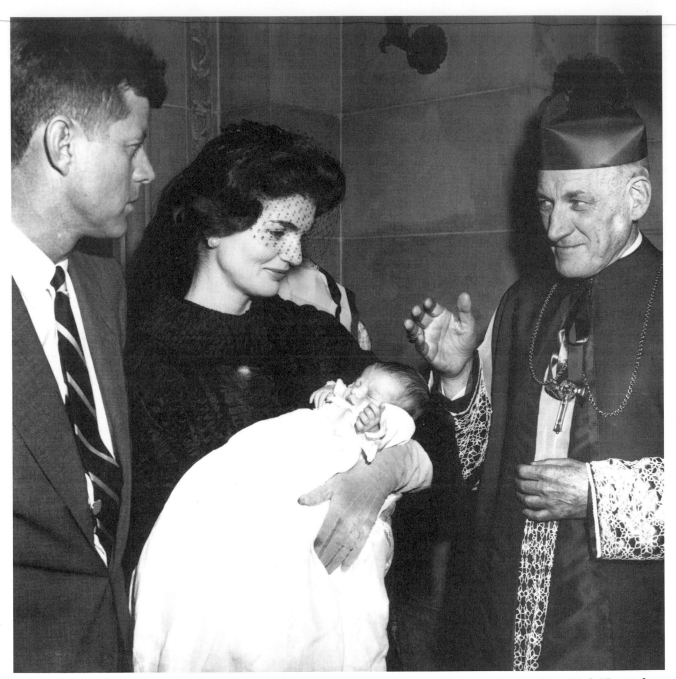

Archbishop Richard Cushing of Boston gives his blessing to Caroline Bouvier Kennedy, born at New York Hospital on November 27 , 1957 .

with her sister."

Jackie canceled the trip three times before summoning up the courage to go. "Jack is always so proud of me when I do something like this," she explained, "but I can't stand being out in front. I know it sounds trite, but what I really want is to be behind him and be a good wife and mother.

She left on the trip wearing her $75,000 leopard skin coat, with an entourage that included her sister, her hairdresser, her personal maid, a press secretary,

her favorite Secret Service man, 24 security guards and 64 pieces of luggage. Traveling 16,000 miles in 20 days, the sisters stopped in Rome for a private audience with Pope John XXIIII. They saw the Taj Mahal by moonlight, visited the Pink City of Jaipur, roamed the Shalimar Gardens of Lahore. They rode elephants in India, camels in Pakistan and sailed down the Holy Ganges.

After the trip, Jackie said, "Lee was just marvelous. It must have been trying sometimes. Though we'd

Mrs. Kennedy and her children during a horseback ride at their estate, Glen Ora, on Nov. 19, 1962. The First Lady and John, Jr. are riding "Sardar" and Caroline is riding "Macaroni."

Jackie, Caroline and unidentified cat.

often ride together, sometimes I'd go ahead with the most interesting person, and Lee would follow along five cars behind and, by the time I got there I couldn't even find her. I was so proud of her—and we would always have such fun laughing about little things when the day was over. Nothing could ever come between us."

In the summer, Jackie went to Hyannisport while the President made state visits to Germany and England and a sentimental journey to Ireland. On Au-

gust 7, she took the children horseback riding in Osterville, a few miles from the Kennedy compound. She began having labor pains on the way home. Her obstetrician, Dr. John Walsh, who was vacationing nearby, arranged for her to be taken to the military hospital at Otis Air Force Base. "Dr. Walsh, you've just got to get me to the hospital on time," Jackie pleaded. "I don't want anything to happen to this baby. Please hurry! This baby mustn't be born dead!"

An hour after she entered the hospital for Cesar-

Princess Grace is greeted by Mrs. Kennedy at the White House May 24, 1961.

ean surgery, the hospital announced that Mrs. John F. Kennedy had given birth to a baby boy weighing four pounds and one-half ounces. The child, born five and a half weeks prematurely, was immediately baptized Patrick Bouvier Kennedy. The President flew in and was told that Jackie was resting nicely, but that the baby had a serious respiratory problem involving the hyaline membrane.

Kennedy wheeled his new son into Jackie's suite and placed the baby in her arms. That night he ac-companied the infant in an ambulance to Boston, where he visited the hospital four times, spending the night on a cot near the infant. Baby Patrick slipped into a coma and died the next day.

"He put up quite a fight," the President told the press, his voice trembling. Then he began to cry. When he broke the news to Jackie, he collapsed in her arms in tears. "Oh, Jack, oh, Jack," she sobbed. "There's only one thing I could not bear now—if I ever lost you." "I know, I know," he murmured.

Vice president Lyndon B. Johnson chats with President and Mrs. Kennedy.

Jackie was too weak to attend the funeral but she insisted that the baby's coffin be covered with flowers, like her father's years before. After the Mass of the Angels, the President placed in the tiny casket the St. Christopher's medal Jackie had given him the day they were married. The baby was buried in Holyrood Cemetery in the Boston suburb of Brookline, a few miles from where the President was born. Kennedy touched the coffin as it was lowered into the ground. "Goodbye," he whispered, tears running down his cheeks. "It's awfully lonely down there."

After the funeral, Jackie seemed to sink into a depression, and the President made a special effort to join her at Hyannis Port every weekend They celebrated their tenth wedding anniversary at Hammersmith Farm. Then Jackie received a phone call from her sis-

ter, who had spent the summer vacationing in Greece with Aristotle Onassis. She had told him how despondent Jackie was after the baby's death, and he had suggested a cruise on his yacht *Christina* to cheer her up. "Tell Jack that Stas and I will chaperone you," she said. "Oh, Jackie, it will be such fun. You can imagine how terrific Ari's yacht is, and he says we can go anywhere you want. It will do you so much good to get away for a while."

Kennedy agreed to let Jackie accept the invitation, although he was concerned about how the press might treat it. Onassis was having an affair with Maria Callas, the opera star. More important, he was under indictment for conspiring to defraud the U. S. Government by using surplus American ships without paying U.S. taxes. He eventually paid a $7 million fine rather

Mrs. Kennedy, wearing a simple black dress and black lace mantilla, stands next to Pope John XXIII during an audience here March 11th. At left is Msgr. Pius A. Benincasa of Buffalo, NY; at right, Msgr. Martin J. O'Connor, Rector of the North American College in Rome.

The perfect First Lady, Jackie Kennedy appears with Charles de Gaulle .

Mrs. Kennedy arrives at Elysee Palace, Paris, 1961 .

The wedding party complete.

Mrs. Kennedy at the Kennedy summer home in Hyannisport, August, 1960.

President Kennedy, governor John Connally of Texas and Mrs. Kennedy ride through Dallas moments before the assassination on Nov. 22, 1963.

than stand trial in the United States.

Onassis, aware of the potential political embarrassment of his invitation, offered to stay in Athens during the cruise, but Jackie insisted he come along. "I could not accept his generous hospitality and then not let him come along," she said later. "It would have been too cruel. I just couldn't have done that." At the President's insistence, Under Secretary of Commerce Franklin D. Roosevelt, Jr., and his wife agreed to go along as informal chaperones.

In addition to Jackie, the Radziwills and Roosevelts, the guests included his sister Artemis and her husband, a Greek playwright, the dress designer Princess Irene Galitzine and her husband, and Accardi Gurney, a good friend of Lee. Onassis stocked the yacht with rare wines, eight varieties of caviar and fresh fruit flown in from Paris. He had a crew of sixty, plus two hairdressers, a Swedish masseuse and a small orchestra for after-dinner dancing.

The *Christina* sailed to Istanbul, where Jackie was cheered by crowds as she walked ashore to see the famous Blue Mosque, then headed for Onassis' dream island of Skorpios. Later a guest said, "Onassis was a wonderful host, very considerate and dynamic, but I can assure you there was nothing between him and Jackie on the cruise. In fact, she kept telling him how wonderful it was to feel so relaxed and said over and over again, 'I just wish Jack could be here with us.'" Kennedy had called by radio-telephone twice during the cruise but the connection was poor and she could barely hear him. She began writing him ten-page letters every night.

The last night at sea, Onassis gave each of the women expensive gifts. Jackie's included a stunning diamond and ruby necklace that could be converted into two bracelets. "Oh, God," gushed Lee Radziwill. "It's so stunning I can't believe it."

Jackie had once told her husband that the country she most wanted to visit was Morocco, and the day after the Onassis cruise ended she did. She arrived with her sister during the celebration honoring the monarch's firstborn son, Prince Mohammed. King Hassan decreed that anything the First Lady admired would be given to her as a gift. When she departed there were three station wagons loaded with presents waiting for her at the airport.

The President was waiting at the airport with the children when she returned to Washington. "Oh, Jack," she said. "I'm so happy to be home."

Jackie, perhaps feeling guilty about the cruise, agreed to accompany her husband to Texas later that month. She made thirteen trips abroad as First Lady, but never made a political trip in the United States. The Texas trip would be her first political trip as first lady, her first outing since the death of little Patrick.

Kennedy was going to Texas to patch up the feud between the conservative Governor, John Connally, and the liberal Senator, Ralph Yarborough, which threatened to give the state to the Republicans in the 1964 election. Even with Lyndon Johnson as his running mate, Kennedy carried Texas in 1960 by only 46,233 votes.

Adlai Stevenson had visited Texas the previous month and had been booed and spat on by angry crowds, and the Secret Service was concerned about possible demonstrations against the President. The White House had announced that the First Lady would accompany Jack on the two day (November 21 and 22) swing through Texas, including fund-raising events in San Antonio, Houston, Fort Worth and Dallas. The Kennedys planned to spend the following weekend at Lyndon Johnson's ranch near Austin, and Jackie promised to be at her husband's side at the round of events. "She will help in every way she can," said the White House spokesman, "consistent with other obligations and continuing good health."

Jackie told her friends, "You know how I hate that sort of thing. But if he wants me there, then that's all that matters. It's a tiny sacrifice on my part for something he feels is very important to him."

The Kennedys board the Presidential jet for their fateful journey to Texas.

Chapter 6

Jackie was late as usual, and Air Force One departed Andrews Air Force Base at 11:05 and headed southwest toward Texas. When it landed at San Antonio, the crowd roared with excitement. Jackie emerged from the plane first, smiling brightly, and received a huge bouquet of yellow roses. In the crowd were hand-lettered signs that read "WELCOME JFK," "JACKIE COME WATER-SKIING IN TEXAS," and "BIENVENIDO MR. AND MRS. PRESIDENT." More crowds cheered the Presidential motorcade, dousing the limousine with confetti. Unaccustomed to so much noisy excitement, Jackie was stiff and tentative. "You see," Kennedy told her reassuringly. "You do make a difference."

In Houston, Jackie was annoyed when Senator Yarborough and Vice President Johnson each refused to ride with the other. She resented Jack having to spend his time arbitrating their differences. She did not like Governor Connally. She did not like the crowds that gawked at her. She was worn out by smiling and waving all day. That night, she came into Jack's hotel room to find that the double mattress had been replaced with a single sleeping board for his bad back. She returned to her own room.

The President left the hotel early the next morning. A crowd had gathered in the rain to greet him. He pointed at the windows of his suite. "Mrs. Kennedy is organizing herself." he said. "It takes her a little longer, but, of course, she looks better than us when she does it" Then he went to a Chamber of Commerce breakfast, telling the 2,000 who filled the hotel ballroom: "Two years ago I introduced myself in Paris by saying that I was the man who accompanied Mrs. Kennedy to Paris. I am getting somewhat the same sensation as I travel around Texas. Why is it nobody wonders what Lyndon and I will be wearing? Jackie finally arrived to join him at the breakfast, wearing her pink Chanel suit and trademark pillbox hat. The crowd went wild, many standing on chairs to applaud her.

An hour later they were on Air Force One heading for Dallas. The President noted a black-bordered advertisement in the Dallas News attacking his administration and labeling him "fifty times a fool" for signing the nuclear test ban treaty. He handed the paper to Jackie, saying "Oh, God, we're really heading into nut country today. You know, last night would have

been a hell of a night to assassinate a President . . . "

As Air Force One landed at Love Field, cheers went up from a boisterous crowd. There was evidence of hostility, though. Someone was holding up a Confederate flag. Here and there were placards that had legends like: "HELP KENNEDY STAMP OUT DEMOCRACY" and "CAN THE CLAN." As Jackie accepted a bouquet of red roses from the Mayor's wife, her husband walked to the fence to start shaking hands.

A motorcade took them to the Trade Mart where Kennedy was scheduled to make a luncheon speech. He and Jackie rode in an open Lincoln convertible with the Connallys. Jackie wanted to use the bubble top to save her hairdo; Jack didn't because it isolated him from the crowd. He stopped the motorcade twice, first to greet a group of children carrying a sign that read: "MR. PRESIDENT. PLEASE STOP AND SHAKE OUR HANDS," then to greet a group of nuns. People were lined twelve deep on the sidewalk as they reached Live Oak Street. "You sure can't say Dallas doesn't love you, Mr. President," said Nellie Connally. "No, you can't," he replied. "No, you can't."

The motorcade inched along through the deafening crowds. Jackie could barely hear anything. She was uncomfortable under the blazing sun. Mrs. Connally pointed to the underpass ahead. "We're almost through. It's just beyond that."

At 1:30 p.m., the Lincoln passed the Texas School Book Depository. From a sixth-floor window of the building, a social misfit named Lee Harvey Oswald, aimed his rifle, tracking the presidential car in the cross hairs of his telescopic sight. Shots rang out, echoing through Dealey Plaza below.

"My God, I'm hit," said the President, clutching his throat. Governor Connally yelled, "They're going to kill us both." Then as if reaching for the top of his head, which was no longer there, the President's hand faltered. He slumped toward Jackie, the blood pouring from his head. She screamed. "My God, what are they doing? My God, they've killed Jack, they've killed my husband . . . Jack, Jack!"

Cradling his bloody head in her lap, Jackie sobbed: "He's dead—They've killed him—Oh, Jack, oh, Jack, I love you." Frantic and disoriented, Jackie began scrambling head-first on to the trunk of the car to get away. In seconds, Jackie's Secret Service agent, Clint

Caisson bearing body of President John F. Kennedy moves up Pennsylvania Avenue.

John F. Kennedy, Jr. places his PT-109 tie clasp at the grave of his dead father in Arlington National Cemetery. Mrs. Kennedy and daughter Caroline watch. The family made this visit on what would have been his 47th birthday.

Hill, reached the moving limousine. He threw himself onto the back of the President's car, climbed up on the trunk, and grasped Jackie's hand, pushing her back into the seat.

The car raced toward Parkland Memorial Hospital six miles away. Jackie cradled her husband in her arms, refusing to let anyone see him. Hospital aides were waiting with stretchers for the President and the Texas Governor, who was badly wounded but still conscious. Clutching her husband, Jackie refused to let him go.

"Please Mrs. Kennedy," begged Clint Hill. "We must get the President to a doctor."

"I'm not going to let him go, Mr. Hill," she sobbed.

"We've got to take him in, Mrs. Kennedy."

"No, Mr. Hill. You know he's dead. Let me alone."

Then the Secret Service man realized what was paralyzing Jackie. He tore off his suit coat and laid it in her lap so she could cover the President's head. The wound was too gory for others to see. Her suit stained with blood, Jackie stumbled into the hospital still holding onto the coat covering the President's head and he was wheeled into the trauma room.

Kennedy aides, gripped by grief, terror and disbelief, began to arrive at the hospital. Vice President and Mrs. Johnson came and Secret Service men, unsure whether their Commander-in-Chief was dead, wondered if they should transfer their allegiance to the Vice President. Reporters fought for telephones. A priest was summoned as doctors began giving President

Mrs. Kennedy walks with her brother-in-law Attorney-General Robert Kennedy during funeral ceremonies for President Kennedy.

Mrs. Kennedy and Attorney General Robert Kennedy watch as the casket of the late President is lowered from a plane after its return November 22, 1963.

Kennedy blood transfusions.

Jackie sat outside the trauma room, chain-smoking cigarettes. She heard someone say "resuscitation," and began to hope that he might still be alive. "I'm going in there," she told a nurse. "I want to be with him when he dies."

She watched her husband receive the last rites of the Roman Catholic Church. She knelt on the blood-soaked floor to pray. "Eternal rest grant unto him, O Lord," murmured the priest, anointing the President's head with oil. "Let perpetual light shine upon him," responded Jackie.

When the bronze casket arrived, the doctors tried to make Jackie leave the room. "Do you think seeing the coffin can upset me, doctor? I've just seen my husband shot and die, in my arms. His blood is all over me. How can I see anything worse than I've seen?" The doctors allowed her to stay. As long-time Kennedy aides and friends Kenny O'Donnell and Dave Powers watched, she slipped her wedding ring off her left hand and placed it on his finger. Then she kissed him on the lips and said good-bye.

As she left the room, she turned to Kenny O'Donnell. "The ring," she said. "Did I do the right thing?" Barely able to speak, O'Donnell said, "You leave it right where it is." He would get the ring back for her later, but now it was imperative to take the President's body back to Washington as quickly as possible. The medical examiner insisted the body be left there for an autopsy according to state law. O'Donnell wanted Jackie spared that ordeal. Kennedy aides and Secret agents lifted the coffin into a waiting hearse and ordered the driver to speed to Love Field.

Aboard Air Force One, someone suggested Jackie change her blood-stained clothes. "No," she whispered fiercely. "Let them see what they have done." She did comb her hair and wash her face. When asked if she wanted to watch Lyndon Johnson take the oath of office, she replied, "I think I ought to. In the light of history, it will be better if I was there." She watched as Federal District Judge Sarah T. Hughes administered the Oath of Office. The ceremony took no more than

President Lyndon B. Johnson flanked by his wife Ladybird and the widowed Jackie is sworn in as President of the United States by Federal District Judge Sarah T. Hughes of Dallas aboard the Presidential plane prior to returning to Washington.

two minutes. Jackie refused to sit with the Johnsons after the swearing-in. She returned to the back of the plane and sat next to her husband's coffin. She kept her vigil throughout the flight back to Washington, her husband's intimates, the Irish Mafia, nearby.

It was during that sad flight that she began to plan her husband's funeral. She vowed that she would make up to him in death what she did not give him in life. "What if I hadn't been there," she said over and over. "I'm so glad I was there." She recalled once asking her husband during their first year in the White House where they would be buried. "Hyannis, I guess," said Kennedy. "We'll all be there." Jackie remembered that she had answered, "Well, I don't think you should be buried in Hyannis. I think you should be buried in Arlington. You just belong to all the country."

President Kennedy's death shattered the nation. Businesses closed, schools recessed, public events were canceled. Throughout the long weekend people watched transfixed in front of their television sets as

the President's life and death flickered on the screen. Television would be their only link to the tragic event that would affect them for the rest of their lives.

They saw the casket containing the body of President John F. Kennedy being carried off Air Force One by his friends. They saw his beautiful young widow emerge on the arm of the Attorney General, still wearing her blood-splattered clothes. "I don't want any undertakers," she said. "I want everything done by the Navy." She recounted to Robert Kennedy in painful detail everything that happened to his beloved brother in Dallas.

Waiting for Jackie at the Bethesda Naval Hospital were the Auchinclosses, Jean Kennedy Smith, Eunice Shriver and other relatives and friends. At the hospital Robert Kennedy learned that Lee Harvey Oswald was being held in Dallas as the assassin. He called Jackie aside and said, "They think they've found the man who did it. They said he's a Communist."

"He didn't even have the satisfaction of being killed

Jackie with Bobby Kennedy at Arlington National Cemetery.

Mrs. Kennedy stands with her children at the May 14, 1965 dedication ceremonies of a memorial to her late husband.

for civil rights," Jackie said. "It had to be some silly little Communist. It even robs his death of any meaning." Controversy would cloud the assassination from that day forward. Jackie would testify before the Warren Commission, but she would never pay any attention to the all the books and reports that questioned whether Lee Harvey Oswald acted alone.

The sad task of telling Caroline fell to Maud Shaw, her British nanny. "I can't help crying, Caroline, because I have some very sad news to tell you. Your father has gone to look after Patrick. Patrick was so lonely in heaven. He didn't know anyone there. Now he has the best friend anybody could have." John-John learned of his father's death. When Maud Shaw explained that he had gone to heaven, the three-year-old asked: "Did he take his big plane with him?" "Yes, John, he probably did," Miss Shaw replied. "I wonder when he's coming back," said the uncomprehending child.

Robert Kennedy took charge of the arrangements. He ordered a catafalque, canon, the military, including the Green Berets, the special forces whom Kennedy had sent to Viet Nam. The East Room was draped in black for the White House memorial service. Kennedy's body would lie in state in the rotunda of the Capitol on Sunday and be buried on Monday after a funeral Mass.

President Johnson addressed the nation. "This is a sad time for all people," he said. "We have suffered a loss that cannot be weighed. I know the world shares the sorrow that Mrs. Kennedy and her family bear. I will do my best. That's all I can do. I ask for your help—and God's."

Jackie did not want to leave the hospital. "I'm not leaving here 'til Jack goes, but I won't cry till it's all over," she said. She refused all sedatives and chain-smoked as she watched television. She begged everyone to stay with her at the White House. "She can't bear to be alone," her mother said. "It's almost as though she doesn't want the day to end," recalled Martha Bartlett.

In the early hours of the morning, Jackie was driven to the White House where she accompanied her husband's coffin up the steps of the North Portico. There she went upstairs and finally took off her stained clothes. She was given a full gram of amytal by Dr. John Walsh and went to sleep.

In the morning, the White House movers began crating Kennedys' office furniture. President Johnson was operating out of the Executive Office Building next door to allow the widow to have the White House as long as she wanted it. She would stay for eleven days.

The Radziwills, arriving from London, remarked on the regal atmosphere that pervaded the White House. "It's just like Versailles when the King died." Stanislas said. It became more so when Jackie insisted that an eternal flame be installed over her husband's grave, like the flame flickering over the Tomb of the Unknown Soldier under the Arc de Triomphe in Paris.

Heads of state were summoned to Washington to walk with the cortege from the White House to the Pontifical Requiem Mass at St. Matthew's Cathedral, then to the final military rites at Arlington National Cemetery. Ninety-two nations sent delegations with Charles de Gaulle leading the way. Later he would say of Jackie, "She gave an example to the whole world of how to behave."

Alone in the Presidential suite, Jackie made endless lists of everything that had to be done, and dispatched memos around the White House. She designed the black-bordered Mass card. She ordered sympathy cards. She selected from the President's personal possessions certain things to give to his aides, friends and family as mementos, which she presented with personal letters. She wrote to the widow of the Dallas policeman shot by Oswald. She insisted that Luigi Vena, the tenor soloist at her wedding, sing the "Ave Maria" at the funeral. She wanted Bunny Mellon to arrange the flowers on the President's grave. She ordered a black veil to cover her face.

She wrote a long letter filled with love and remorse to her dead husband. She told Caroline, "You must write a letter to Daddy now, and tell him how much you love him." Caroline printed in block letters, "Dear Daddy: We are all going to miss you. Daddy, I love you very much. Caroline." Too young to write his own letter, John-John marked Caroline's letter with an X. Jackie took the letters, a piece of the President's scrimshaw, a pair of his gold cufflinks which she had given him and placed them all in his coffin. Lee Radziwill added two sapphire bracelets, and Robert Kennedy his gold PT-boat tie clasp. They looked on as Jackie cut a lock of hair from the slain President's head.

As the world watched on television, Jackie left the White House with her two children to visit the flag-draped coffin of her husband lying in state under the Capitol dome. Senator Mike Mansfield who gave the eulogy, remembered " . . . and so she took a ring from her finger and placed it in his hands, and kissed him and closed the lid of a coffin . . ." Jackie approached the bier, holding the white-gloved hand of her little

Little John F. Kennedy, Jr. stands by his mother, Mrs. Kennedy, and his sister, Caroline, saluting as the casket containing the remains of President Kennedy leaves St. Matthew's Cathedral November 25, 1963. Behind Caroline is Senator Edward M. Kennedy, and behind little John is Attorney General Robert F. Kennedy.

Mrs. Kennedy waits with her brothers-in-law, Sen. Edward Kennedy, and Attorney General Robert F. Kennedy in the latter's office in the Justice Department to making her first public statement after her husband's assassination.

blonde daughter. "We're going to say good-bye to Daddy and we're going to kiss him good-bye, and tell Daddy how much we love him and how much we'll always miss him," she whispered to Caroline.

As tears blurred the eyes of millions, they rose to approach the coffin. Jacqueline Kennedy became a national folk heroine. Here legend began as she appeared in front of the White House to lead the funeral procession to St. Matthew's Cathedral. The cadence of muffled drums, the booming twenty-one gun salutes, the solemn marchers and the clatter of the hoofs of the riderless horse were burned into the consciousness of everyone who watched on that bright November day.

Holding the hands of her children, both dressed in light-blue coats and red lace-up shoes, she stood erect, listening reverently to Cardinal Cushing's prayers and seemed touched when he slipped from the traditional Latin to English, crying out, "May the angels, dear Jack, lead you into Paradise."

As the cortege began the final march from the cathedral to Arlington, the band saluted the dead President with a final rendition of "Hail to the Chief." As the soldiers in the parade saluted their fallen leader, Jackie bent over and whispered to her son, "John, you can salute Daddy now and say good-bye."

The little boy stepped forward, raised his right hand stiffly and cocked his elbow at precisely the right angle. The image of John-John giving his father a final salute broke the heart of the nation. No one who saw the small saddened face of John Fitzgerald Kennedy, Jr. as he said good-bye to his father would ever forget it or remember it without a catch in their throat.

Wearing the same black suit she wore when her husband announced his Presidential candidacy, Jackie lit the eternal flame over his grave and passed the torch to his brothers. She returned to the White House past people sobbing in the streets. There she presided over a reception for the visiting heads of state. She was emotionally spent with only nervous energy to keep her going. After all the state visitors had departed, she gathered her family and friends in the private dining room to celebrate the birthdays of Caroline and John-John.

On Thanksgiving Jackie flew to Hyannisport to see Joe Kennedy, who was not allowed to attend his son's funeral. She brought the paralyzed patriarch the flag that lay over John F. Kennedy's coffin. She walked into his room, put her arms around him and said, "Grandpa, Jack's gone and nothing will ever be the same again for us. He's gone and I want to tell you about it." For more than an hour the thirty-four-year old widow poured out her heart to her father-in-law, reliving the most harrowing experience of her life.

She returned to the White House two days later to begin packing. Suddenly alone and frightened, she clung to her staff for support. Weeping, she turned to her personal secretary, Mary Gallagher. "Why did Jack have to die so young: Even when you're sixty, you like to know your husband is there. It's so hard for the children. Please, Mary, don't ever leave. Get yourself fixed for salary on my government appropriation—just don't leave me." "Mr. West," she said to the White House usher, "will you be my friend for life?"

The White House she once detested now was her home, and she dreaded leaving it. The day before her departure she ordered an inscribed bronze plaque placed over the fireplace in the President's bedroom. It read: "In this room lived John Fitzgerald Kennedy with his wife Jacqueline—during the 2 years, 10 months and 2 days he was President of the United States—January 20, 1961—November 22, 1963."

No other First Lady in history had memorialized her husband that way. Only one other such plaque existed, and that was the one on the President's mantel which read: "In this room Abraham Lincoln slept during his occupancy at the White House as President of the United State, March 4, 1861—April 13, 1864. Jackie had her plaque placed right beneath that of Abraham Lincoln.

Chapter 7

Jackie proclaimed a year of mourning for herself and would spend it enshrining the memory of her husband. Before leaving the White House, she asked President Johnson to rededicate Cape Canaveral in Florida to him so that when American astronauts reached the moon they would arrive in a rocket from Cape Kennedy. On St. Patrick's Day, March 17, she placed shamrocks on her husband's grave and mailed 900,000 black-bordered prayer cards to acknowledge the sympathy cards she had received.

She told Theodore H. White, author and a Kennedy confident, that the title song of the musical "Camelot" had become "an obsession with me" lately. She said that at night before bedtime, her husband had often played it, or asked her to play it, on an old Victorola in their bedroom. White quoted her as saying: "And the song he loved most came at the very end of this record, the last side of Camelot, sad Camelot . . . 'Don't let it be forgot, that once there was a spot, for one brief shining moment, that was known as Camelot.' '. . . There'll never be another Camelot again."

White later recalled: "So the epitaph on the Kennedy Administration became Camelot—a magic moment in American history, when gallant men danced with beautiful women, when great deeds were done, when writers and poets met at the White House and the barbarians beyond the walls were held back."

She told her friends that she would live in Washington to pursue the dreams of Camelot. "I'm never going to live in Europe," she said. "I'm not going to travel extensively abroad. I'm going to live in the places I lived with Jack. In Georgetown and with the Kennedys at the Cape. They're my family. I'm going to bring up my children. I want John to grow up to be a good boy."

She worked on the John F. Kennedy Memorial Library in Boston, opening exhibits and sponsoring displays. She encouraged more than a hundred people associated with the New Frontier to record their recollections, and cooperated with William Manchester in documenting the death of her husband for a book he was writing. She appeared on television to thank the hundreds of thousands of people who wrote to her, and after the broadcast more than a million condolence letters poured in. In less than a year she raised more then $10 million to honor her husband's memory.

The Senate approved a bill to establish the John F. Kennedy Center for the Performing Arts in Washington. New York renamed Idlewild Airport in Kennedy's memory. Across the country cities and towns dedicated an avenue, a school or a square to him. A Kennedy fifty-cent piece was issued. Memorials were dedicated around the world: Corso Kennedy in Rome, Avenue Kennedy in Paris, Kennedy Platz in Berlin. His boyhood home in Brookline, Massachusetts, was made a national historical monument. Congress allocated Jackie a $10,000 a year widow's pension, $50,000 a year to staff her office and continued Secret Service for her and the children for the rest of their lives.

None of this filled the emptiness in her life. "I'm a living wound. My life is over. I'm dried up. I have nothing more to give and some days I can't even get out of bed," she said. "I cry all day and all night until I'm so exhausted I can't function. Then I drink."

Jackie felt beset by financial worries. People assumed that Kennedy's widow inherited millions upon his death. Actually, she only received a lump sum payment of $25,000, plus all her husband's personal effects. She was paid an additional $43,299.26, which represented the total due the President's estate from Navy retirement pay, Civil Service death benefits and the salary owed him as President for November 1-22, 1963. Although Kennedy was the wealthiest man ever to occupy the White House, his taxable assets at the time of his death totaled only $1,890,640.45. Kennedy had established two trust funds for Jackie and the children. They were valued at $10 million, but Jackie's share as a widow was limited to yearly payments from the principal of one trust.

Two months after the assassination, she met with the Kennedy family financial advisor. Afterward she began receiving $200,000 a year from the trust fund. She continued to send her bills to the Kennedy office in New York, which handled everything for her. Yet Jackie, who could spent $40,000 in department stores in three months, continued to worry about money.

After the first year, a friend observed, Jackie was "wandering around looking like the survivor of an airplane crash." Finally Lee Radziwill persuaded her sister to move to New York, where she would not be such a tourist attraction. "You've got to get out of this gloomy

Crowds line both sides of the bridge as the 325 ft. white yacht "Christina"—with honeymooners Jacqueline and Aristotle aboard—crosses into the Epripos Straits in Khalkis, Greece.

Aristotle Onassis and bride, Jackie Kennedy, talk to reporters October 20th after their wedding on Onassis' private island, Skorpios. Caroline Kennedy, 10, stands next to her mother

Aristotle and Jacqueline Onassis chat with guests at a party hosted by Dr. Reza Fallah.

city," she said. "Washington is too full of painful memories for you." She bought a five-bedroom cooperative apartment at 1040 Fifth avenue for $200,000.

Jackie worked hard at making a new life. She skiied in Vermont, sailed in the West Indies, cruised with friends, shopped in New York, entertained old friends. She tried to do the things that other Fifth Avenue mothers did, walking her children to school, attending their plays and concerts, taking them on the carousel in Central Park, buying them ice cream from the Good Humor truck. She did all she could to help Bobby

campaign for his Senate seat in New York. No matter what she did, though, she still was haunted by death. "I can't escape it," she said. "Whether I'm helping with the Kennedy Memorial at Harvard, or taking a plane from Kennedy Airport, or seeing a Kennedy in-law, I always think of Jack and what they did to him."

When the official period of mourning was over, Jackie shed her widow's weeds and increased her social activities. She refused to attend President Johnson's Inaugural ceremonies, but went to Mexico and later vacationed with her sister and the children at Hobe

Wearing mod sunglasses and a miniskirt, Jacqueline Kennedy Onassis accompanies her husband, Aristotle, to a plane at Kennedy Airport, June 5, 1969 before the Greek shipping magnate took off for Athens.

Aristotle and Jacqueline Onassis pause for a rest during their 10-day tour of Egypt, March 28, 1974.

Sound, Florida. The Johnsons invited her for the dedication of the Rose Garden in her honor; she sent her mother instead. A few weeks later she flew to England for Queen Elizabeth's dedication of Runnymede in memory of Kennedy. She attended the New York opening of "Leonard Bernstein's Theater Songs." She celebrated her 36th birthday with the Kennedys in Hyannisport. That August she vacationed in Newport, Rhode Island. She attended balls in Boston and New York and threw a large party for John Kenneth Galbraith, Kennedy's Ambassador to India. She leased a country home in New Jersey's fox-hunting area. She spent the second anniversary of the assassination alone in her apartment, refusing to watch television or read the newspapers, then went to Hammersmith farm to celebrate Thanksgiving and the children's birthdays.

To some, Jackie fell from grace as the year of mourn-ing ended. She was photographed wearing a miniskirt. She was seen in the company of such prominent bachelors as Frank Sinatra, Marlon Brando and Mike Nichols. She toured the Saville Fair in Spain sporting a crimson jacket and a rakish broad-brimmed hat, tossing down a glass of sherry. She was young, attractive and apparently wanted to live her life with brio.

In December, Jackie made a secret trip to Washington to stand in the rain as Cardinal Cushing blessed the new resting place at Arlington for her husband. Next to his grave now were the two deceased children.

As President Johnson emerged from the shadow of John F. Kennedy he quickly fell from Jackie's favor. Tension reached the point where she was complaining bitterly about "that goddamned Lyndon." She said that she would rather return to Dallas than return to Washington while Johnson was in the White House.

Jackie and Ari at Skorpios Oct. 20, 1968, after their wedding.

Mrs. Jacqueline Kennedy Onassis and her two children, Caroline and John F. Kennedy, Jr. arrive in New York, from Athens, Greece, after spending a Christmas holiday on the Onassis yacht in the Aegean Sea.

Jacqueline Onassis

Accompanied by her sister, Princess Lee Radziwill, Jacqueline Kennedy stands by the coffin of her brother-in-law, the late Sen. Robert F. Kennedy, in St. Patrick's Cathedral June 8, 1968. In center is the Rev. Ralph Abernathy.

Jackie also acted as the guardian of her husband's image. She made Paul Fay delete thousands of words from his book *The Pleasure of His Company*. Later he sent her a $3,000 check for the Kennedy Library. She sent it back. Because of his book, she never spoke to him again. "She cooperated with Ted Sorenson and Arthur Schlesinger, Jr., on their Kennedy books," said one of her aides, "but she insisted that she be referred to only as Jacqueline or Mrs. Kennedy—never Jackie. You'll notice in both books that her marriage to JFK is described in loving terms, and never once do they hint at the painful truth behind that relationship."

The big problem came with William Manchester's book, *The Death of a President*. His contract gave the Kennedys full right of review and revision before pub-

lication. Jackie objected to the unkind references to her vanity and candid descriptions of events in Jack and her public and private life.

Look bought the serial rights to the book. First, Bobby wanted publication delayed to fit his political plans and the magazine agreed. Then Jackie decided she didn't want the book published or serialized. She pressured the publishers and threatened to sue. She summoned Manchester to Hyannisport and tried to prevail on their friendship to withdraw the book. She told Manchester, "Anyone who is against me will look like a rat unless I run off with Eddie Fisher."

Manchester was hospitalized for nervous exhaustion. He had spent two years of his life writing the book. Now he was being asked to rewrite history and forfeit

Angkor Wat, Nov. 24, 1967.

Bright-eyed Jacqueline Kennedy visits New York campaign headquarters of Sen. Robert F. Kennedy late May 7, 1968 after it was apparent that he had won the Indiana preferential Presidential primary.

Jacqueline Kennedy Onassis and her son, John F. Kennedy, Jr., along with some of his friends, visit Palisades Amusement Park May 5, 1969, on an afternoon outing.

serialization, which would be the only profit he could ever make.

When it was all over, the book earned more than a million dollars, all of which went to the John F. Kennedy Memorial Library. Manchester's taped interview with Jackie, 313 minutes long, was sealed for one-hundred years and is scheduled to be opened in the year 2067.

The free-for-all over the book cost Jackie more than she won. The passages that she demanded be deleted found their way into the press around the world, and public opinion suddenly shifted against her. For five consecutive years she had topped the Gallup poll as the woman in the world most Americans admired. Now they saw that she had feet of clay. At the insistence of the Kennedys, she forfeited the federal money that had

been appropriated to maintain her office. She became even more secretive. Friends who even mentioned her name to a reporter became enemies. Employees were bound to silence by legal affidavits. She fired her chef when she learned he was planning to publish a cookbook.

Jackie's silence about her past, especially about the Kennedy years and her marriage to the President, was always something of a mystery. Her family never spoke of it. Either out of loyalty or trepidation over her wrath, her closest friends shed no light on it, and there was nothing authoritative to be learned beyond her inner circle.

Aristotle Onassis continued to be a close friend of Jackie's throughout her mourning. He would visit her in her Manhattan apartment, bringing gifts for her and

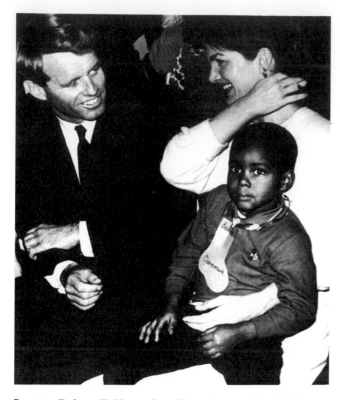

Senator Robert F. Kennedy, talks to Jacqueline, holding four-year-old Bobby Johnson, at the Senator's party for underprivileged children at the Hodgson Center.

the children. She enjoyed his company but refused to go out in public. Meanwhile, Bobby Kennedy was planning to run for President in 1968, and the idea of Jackie marrying Onassis was unthinkable. At his insistence, she agreed to do nothing for five months.

The issue in 1968 was President Johnson's escalation of the war in Viet Nam. He was challenged by Eugene McCarthy, who was so successful in the early primaries that Johnson was forced to withdraw his candidacy. Bobby entered the race, expecting McCarthy to step aside but he refused and the Democratic primaries became bitter contests.

All the Kennedys actively campaigned for Bobby except Jackie. She told Arthur Schlesinger, Jr. that she hoped "Bobby would never become President . . ." Asked why, she said, "If he becomes President, they'll do to him what they did to Jack."

On June 5, 1968, Robert Francis Kennedy was shot in the Ambassador Hotel in Los Angeles, minutes af-

ter he won the California primary. At 3:45 a.m. the phone rang in Jackie's New York apartment. Stanislaus Radziwill was calling from Long Island. "Jackie," he said, "how's Bobby?"

"He's fine. Terrific," she said. "You heard that he won California by 53 percent, didn't you?"

"Yes, but how is he?"

"I just told you. He won California."

"But Jackie, he's been shot. It happened just a few minutes ago."

"No. It can't have happened," she screamed. "Not again!"

Jackie immediately flew to Los Angeles to stand with Ethel as Bobby fought for life. When he was pronounced dead, she wept until she was exhausted. President Johnson sent a White House plane to bring Bobby's body back home.

Jackie had Leonard Bernstein make arrangements for music at the funeral in St. Patrick's Cathedral. Ethel wanted the nuns from her alma mater, Manhattanville College to sing, and to have Andy Williams sing "The Battle Hymn of the Republic," both considerably unsuitable, but Jackie intervened with Cardinal Spellman and he gave in.

The funeral stressed the Resurrection. It was in English and the vestments were violet instead of black. The Kennedy children, dressed in white, carried the Communion articles to the altar. Teddy, the last Kennedy brother, delivered the eulogy. In a voice that often broke, he described his dead brother as "a good man who saw wrong and tried to right it, saw suffering and tried to heal it, saw war and tried to stop it." A funeral train carried Robert Kennedy's body to Washington to be buried alongside his brother in Arlington National Cemetery.

"Jackie was very bitter after Bobby's death," a Kennedy aide recalled. "She became quite hysterical at one point and said, 'I hate this country. I despise America, and I don't want my children to live here any more. If they are killing Kennedys, my kids are the number one targets.' "

Jackie was in a state of shock. The strong support of her brother-in-law was gone. Her father-in-law was in a wheelchair unable to talk. She felt alone and unprotected. There was no one to lean on now, no one to turn to for help.

Mrs. Jacqueline Kennedy and her escort Alan Jay Lerner, go backstage after a performance of
"On A Clear Day You Can See Forever."

Mrs. Kennedy prays for her slain brother-in-law, Robert F. Kennedy, in St. Patrick's Cathedral in New York, June 7, 1968.

Chapter 8

After the funeral, Jackie phoned Aristotle Onassis and invited him and his daughter to spend the weekend with her and her family at Hammersmith Farm. "Mummy almost died," Jamie Auchincloss recalled. "She was absolutely fit to be tied. She couldn't believe it. When Onassis arrived, Mummy treated him very badly." Janet Auchincloss was disgusted that Jackie would turn to Onassis in her grief, but she had no idea that she would soon want to turn to the sixty-two-year-old Greek for the rest of her life.

Throughout the summer, Onassis visited Jackie in Hyannisport, getting to know Caroline and John and the rest of the Kennedys. He particularly liked Rose and her many eccentricities. Rose found him charming but not very attractive. Teddy accepted Ari's invitation to escort Jackie on a cruise on the *Christina*. He wanted to convince Ari not to propose to Jackie. Failing that, he wanted to discuss the financial future of Jackie and the children.

Aristotle Socrates Onassis was one of the richest men in the world. And one of the most notorious. He sailed his ships under foreign flags to escape taxes and buried his business dealings in questionable corporations. He had been arrested in the Unites States in 1954, indicted on criminal charges, and paid a $7 million fine to avoid a trial. He flaunted his love affair with Maria Callas, who left her Italian husband to follow Onassis around the world. Later Onassis was sued for divorce by his wife, Tina. Newspapers were full of the shipping magnate and the opera singer, their melodramatic fights, separations and reconciliations.

What few knew was that in the Spring of 1968, Onassis and Callas were about to get married. At the last minute they quarreled violently, and he stormed out. Soon after, Ari began seeing Jackie regularly in New York. Apparently, Jackie felt secure with Onassis, who in many ways resembled her father-in-law. She began to confide in him. She told him how difficult it was to be emotionally and financially shackled to the Kennedys. In the early days of their courtship, Onassis felt compassion for her and wanted to brighten her life. He felt needed. For Jackie, he was the only man she knew who could offer her the protection and security she so desperately wanted.

There were obstacles to their marriage. Onassis, a divorced man, was a member of the Greek Orthodox Church. As a Roman Catholic, Jackie would risk excommunication if she married him. She did not want the Vatican to denounce the union, if only for the sake of the children. And she needed to prepare the Kennedys. But she was determined to marry Onassis, come what may.

Onassis had problems, too. Christina and Alexander loved their mother and resented any other woman in their father's life. They despised Callas, blaming her for the divorce which separated their parents. Although he was estranged from his children, he did not want to rob them of what little emotional security they had.

Under Greek law, the husband was required to leave at least 12.5 percent of his wealth to his wife and 37.5 percent to his children. This meant that if they married Jackie stood to inherit $64 million of his estimated $500 million estate. Onassis wanted to take care of Jackie financially, but not at the expense of his children. He asked her to waive her inheritance right in return for $3 million for herself and a million each for Caroline and John. He and Teddy worked this out during the cruise.

The Kennedy family tried its best to keep Jackie from marrying Onassis. Jackie took her case to Cardinal Cushing, who gave her his full support, despite the Kennedy protests. He assured her that their meetings would remain as confidential as a confessional. At the Kennedy compound over Labor Day weekend, matters came to a head. Everyone, including Teddy, was upset, but they finally accepted the inevitable. They made Jackie promise that Caroline and John would be educated and raised in the United States no matter how much time she spent abroad.

On October 15th, the Boston *Herald-Traveler* ran a front-page story predicting Jackie and Onassis would be married in the near future. Jackie phoned Onassis to tell him the story was out and that they should be married as soon as possible. Then she phoned her mother to ask her to announce the engagement. Her mother, who did not realize she and Ari were serious, was hysterical. "She's finally getting back at me for divorcing her father," Lee Auchincloss told a friend. "That's what she's doing. I just know it." She finally agreed to make the announcement, and attend the wedding.

Mrs. Kennedy, accompanied by her children Caroline and John, Jr., appear on horseback. Mrs. Kennedy was in Ireland on a six-week holiday.

On October 17, 1968, an announcement was made in New York to the press. Nancy Tuckerman, who still handled Jackie's press relations, said, "Mrs. Hugh D. Auchincloss has asked me to tell you that her daughter, Mrs. John F. Kennedy, is planning to marry Aristotle Onassis sometime next week." No place or date has been set for the moment.

It was a field day for the tabloids, a shock to members of Jackie's family, and a puzzlement to the public, who still treasured the Camelot-Kennedy mystique. The prospective bridegroom was much shorter and more than twenty-eight years older, and not even an American.

That afternoon, Jackie and the children left her Fifth Avenue apartment and accompanied by her friend Bunny Mellon and a group of Secret Service men en-

tered a limousine for the airport. There she met her mother and Hugh Auchincloss, Jean Kennedy Smith, and Pat Kennedy Lawford and her daughter. Onassis had arranged for the wedding party to fly on his airline, Olympic Airways, and had bumped ninety scheduled passengers so that they could have a plane to themselves for the flight to Greece.

News of the coming marriage shocked the world. "JACKIE, HOW COULD YOU?" asked the Stockholm *Expression*. "SHE'S NO LONGER A SAINT," said Oslo's *Verdens Gang*. Everyone had an opinion. Few approved of Jack Kennedy's widow marrying an aging Greek millionaire of questionable character. The press nicknamed her "Jackie O." The name stuck.

Jackie and Ari were married on the afternoon of

Mrs. Kennedy and daughter, Caroline, and son, John-John, walk to plane en route to Gstaad, Switzerland, on a skiing holiday.

Mrs. Jacqueline Onassis, followed by her husband, Aristotle Onassis, and her son, John F. Kennedy' Jr., leaving Manhattan's Plaza Hotel following luncheon at Trader Vic's restaurant, Feb. 16, 1969.

Jacqueline Onassis and her son John F. Kennedy, Jr. leave the school chapel at Brown University where John received a Bachelor's Degree in history.

October 20, 1968, on the Greek island of Skorpios. A light rain was falling, a good omen at Greek weddings. She entered the small chapel wearing a beige chiffon and lace two-piece Valentino dress with long sleeves that fell three inches above her knees. Despite her low-heeled shoes, the five-foot-seven bride towered over the bridegroom. John Jr. and Caroline stood next to their mother holding ceremonial candles.

Hugh Auchincloss gave his step-daughter in marriage as he had fifteen years before when she wed John F. Kennedy. A bearded Greek Orthodox priest clad in gold brocade performed the thirty-minute ceremony. He intoned: "Do Thou now, Master, send down Thine hand from Thy holy dwelling place and unite Thy servants, Aristotle and Jacqueline, for by Thee woman is united to man."

Onassis had gone to great lengths to protect his bride's privacy. Two helicopters equipped with bullhorns guarded the island. A security force of 200 armed men held back the mob of reporters and photographers. Patrol boats, reinforced by cruisers and helicopters from the Greek navy, circled the island to keep the press from getting too close.

After the ceremony was over, the couple posed briefly for the photographers. The pictures showed a serenely smiling thirty-nine-year-old bride, her hand through the arm of the slouching sixty-two year old groom. Caroline and John, Jr. were not smiling. Neither were Onassis's children, Alexander and Christina.

Jeeps took the wedding party to the *Christina* where the wedding party changed clothes for the reception and dinner. They were stunned by Onassis's sea palace. The yacht, longer than a football field, had a crew of fifty, and nine guest rooms and suites, each with a marble bathroom with solid gold fixtures. The owners quarters were at the top of a circular staircase. In the large study was a painting by El Greco, valued at $2.5 million. The bedroom was adorned with 18th century Venetian mirrors. A mirror lined dressing room led into a marble bathroom that resembled a temple.

Among the yacht's amenities were a small movie theater, a grand piano and a fireplace in the smoking room, and a swimming pool decorated with a reproduction of a mosaic from the Minos palace. The bottom of the pool could be raised to deck level and used as a dance floor. The yacht's hospital had surgical and X-ray equipment. The yacht carried eight speedboats, two lifeboats, three dinghies, one sailboat, two kayaks, one glass-bottom boat and a hydroplane. There were forty-two phones and an intercom system to allow guests to ring for maids, valets, seamstresses and masseuses. Basic operating costs totaled $1,140,000 a year. "My God," exclaimed Pat Lawford. "I can't quite believe it."

Jackie came to dinner in a floor-length white skirt, a black blouse and the gold bejeweled caftan belt that the King of Morocco gave her while she was First Lady. On the third finger of her left hand was a cabochon ruby the size of an Easter egg, surrounded by dozens of one-caret diamonds. Dangling from her ears were heart-shaped rubies framed in diamonds. The guests were

Mrs. Jacqueline Kennedy and New York Philharmonic conductor Leonard Bernstein arrive at the gala invitational preview of Martin Ransohoff's "The Sandpiper," in New York City.

Jackie Onassis shares a comment with her son, John F. Kennedy, Jr. as the two leave St. Matthew's Cathedral after the June 9, 1990 wedding of Kerry Kennedy and Andrew Cuomo; at the left is her companion Maurice Templesman.

Jacqueline Kennedy Onassis shows Raisa Gorbachev a book of paintings that she presented to Mrs. Gorbachev during a visit by Mrs. Gorbachev and her husband, former Soviet President Mikhail Gorbachev, to the John F. Kennedy Presidential Library in Boston, May 15, 1992.

Facing Central Park, on the northeast corner of Fifth Avenue and 85th Street, is 1040 Fifth Avenue, the address where Jackie lived in New York.

stunned by the display of more than a million dollars worth of jewelry. Caroline ran up to her mother and broke the silence. "Mummy, mummy, mummy," she cried. "They're so pretty—you're so pretty."

At the wedding dinner Jackie and Ari cut their cake with an antique Greek knife. The children were sent to bed. The adults had after-dinner drinks and danced. The newlyweds sat, holding hands, looking at each other from time to time and smiling. They never kissed.

The next day Ari flew to Athens on business and the guests prepared to fly home. Jackie phoned Billy Baldwin, the New York decorator, to fly over to redo the Skorpios house in time for Christmas. Onassis gave him complete freedom, asking only for a long sofa by the fireplace. The cost of the redecoration was $250,000.

Jackie's picture was on the cover of *Time* and *Newsweek*. Stories described her luxurious new life at Skorpios with seventy-two servants. When she tired

of that, there was the villa in Glyfada with ten servants, a penthouse in Paris with five servants, a hacienda in Montevideo with thirty-eight servants, and a Fifth Avenue apartment in New York with five. All the stories emphasized Ari's money and Jackie's love of it.

A steward on Onassis's yacht wrote a book claiming that he saw a 170-page marriage contract, stipulating separate bedrooms, a $585,040 annual allowance for Jackie while they were married, plus a $20-million settlement in the event of a divorce. Even Jackie's closest friends assumed it was true.

"It's a lie, a complete lie," she told Truman Capote. "I don't have any money. When I married Ari, my income from the Kennedy estate stopped, and so did my widow's pension from the U.S. government. I didn't make any premarital financial agreement with Ari. I know it's an old Greek custom, but I couldn't do it. I didn't want to barter myself. Except for personal possessions, I have exactly $5,200 in a bank account. Everything else I charge to Olympic Airlines."

The truth was that Jackie, for the first time in her life, was rich, truly rich. There were trips and vacations and cruises around the world. The accommodations were deluxe, the suites filled with flowers and champagne. There were limousines and private planes to take her anywhere she wanted to go and international celebrities to amuse her. Ari showered her with jewelry, fur coats, valuable paintings—any material thing her heart desired. She could go on wild spending sprees and shop without accounting to anyone for anything. She didn't bother with cash. Her face was her credit card. The bills were sent to the Onassis office. He could afford her compulsions.

What Onassis couldn't do was protect Jackie from the tragedies that awaited them. Ari's sister died suddenly, his first wife died mysteriously. His only son, Alexander, was killed. Teddy Kennedy missed the bridge at Chappaquiddick and the young woman with him drowned. Teddy's son was stricken with cancer and his leg had to be amputated. Joe Kennedy died. Stas Radziwill died. Cardinal Cushing died. Christina Onassis attempted suicide. Their marriage drifted toward divorce. Then Ari would die and she would be a widow again.

Chapter 9

A month after the wedding, Jackie flew home to be with her children. Ari was in Athens working on the biggest deal of his career, a $400-million investment package for the Greek government. The Greek junta fell, negotiations collapsed, but Ari went ahead with plans to build a shipyard, oil refinery, an aluminum plant, an air terminal and a chain of tourist resorts. The project would revolutionize Greece and make him the richest man in the world.

He flew to New York to spend the weekend with his new family at Jackie's rented country estate in Peapack, New Jersey. Shortly before he arrived, Jackie had a photographer arrested for trespassing and put up barricades on the road that led from the highway to her house. Ari kidded her about turning her place into an armed camp.

In December, Jackie went to Washington to see Ethel Kennedy, who had given birth to her eleventh child. She visited the graves of Jack and their children at Arlington. With Caroline and John Jr., she flew to Greece to be with Ari for Christmas. She gave him a painting of herself; he gave her $300,000 earrings. During the next few years he would shower her with more than $3 million worth of gifts. On her fortieth birthday he gave her a forty-carat diamond and a diamond necklace and bracelet.

After Christmas, Jackie and the children flew back to New York, and Ari flew to Paris where he dined with Maria Callas. The next month he met Jackie in New York to spend some time with Caroline and John before leaving on a cruise to the Canary Islands. Easter was spent cruising on the *Christina* with the children, Rose Kennedy and Nancy Tuckerman, who now was on the Onassis payroll continuing her secretarial duties for Jackie. On the cruise, Ari gave Rose a gold bracelet with a serpent's head studded with diamonds and rubies. Jackie had become closer to Rose since the marriage. "When I married Ari," Jackie said, "she of all people was the one who encouraged me. She said, 'He's a good man.'"

Rose was concerned about her grandchildren. Caroline never fully accepted Onassis as her stepfather. John got along better with him, but he too felt that Onassis was trying to buy their affection. Ari, however, seemed genuinely fond of them, and spent as much time with them as his schedule would allow.

Jackie spent much of her time flying back and forth to Europe. She took the children to join Ari on holidays. Ari would stay on to tend to his business empire. A pattern of separate lives developed, which suited Jackie, who couldn't bear to be with someone for a sustained period. Ari made no demands. He allowed her the freedom to live alone with her children.

"Jackie is a little bird that needs its freedom as well as its security," he told an interviewer, "and she gets both from me. She can do exactly as she pleases—visit international shows and travel and go out with friends to the theater or any place. And I, of course, will do exactly as I please. I never question her and she never questions me."

When Jackie was in New York without Ari, she would call on old friends to escort her. She was frequently seen at social events with Andre Meyer, Bill Walton, Franklin D. Roosevelt, Jr., and Paul Mathias. No longer restrained by the Kennedy clan, she began having fun. She flaunted her new wealth, the expensive jewelry. She became a pacesetter and was voted into the Best Dressed Hall of Fame. She was photographed in tight pants, T-shirts without a bra, calypso skirts, big floppy hats. On Skorpios a photographer managed to film her wearing nothing at all. Publications paid small fortunes to print her nude pictures.

A smiling Jacqueline Onassis poses beside a painting of patriot Paul Revere by John Singleton Copley, noted 18th century American artist, as she attended a special viewing of "Paul Revere's Boston: 1735-1880" exhibit at the Museum of Fine Arts.

Members of the Kennedy family during a press conference May 25, 1989, at the John F. Kennedy Library to announce the John F. Kennedy Profile in Courage Award, an annual $40,000 prize to honor the late President.

Jacqueline Kennedy Onassis shares a laugh with Mikhail Gorbachev, as the two sit together at a lunch held in Gorbachev's honor at the John F. Kennedy Presidential Library in Boston, May 15, 1992.

Jacqueline Kennedy Onassis brushes a wisp of hair from her face as she takes part in a ceremony in Brooklyn on June 20, 1989, at which the Municipal Art Society honored ten visionary individuals and organizations for their outstanding civic achievements.

Caroline Kennedy graduated from Radcliffe at a joint session during Harvard University's 329th Commencement. The family was there to offer congratulations.

Jackie liked publicity but wanted it on her terms. Prying photographers made her furious. One took her picture as she left a movie theater where the pornographic film "I Am Curious Yellow" was playing. She used judo to flip him to the ground.

She particularly disliked Ron Galella, an aggressive paparazzo photographer. She had him arrested for harassing her. Galella filed a $1.3 million countersuit which charged Jackie with assault, false arrest, malicious persecution and interfering with his work. She countersued him for $6 million in damages for invasion of privacy and mental anguish. She was able to get a court order temporarily restraining him from "alarming and frightening" her. She claimed she was an "absolute prisoner" of him and his camera. Ironically, all of Galella's thousands of pictures of Jackie showed her looking beautiful. He never photographed her smoking or drinking. He took pictures in a bright light to camouflage her gray teeth and soften the wrinkles around her eyes.

The court case dragged on. Finally, the judge, a Kennedy appointee, ruled in Jackie's favor. He ordered Galella to stay fifty yards away from Jackie and a hundred yards from her apartment. An appeals court cut the distance to twenty-five feet. Jackie told her friend, "It served him right. He had no right to harass me the way he does." Ari, apparently, didn't agree. He refused to pay Jackie's lawyers their $235,000 fee. "I had nothing to do with the damn thing," he said.

Ari loved Caroline and John, Jr. He indulged their every desire. When Jackie told him that Caroline had her heart set on a particular horse, Ari cut her off in mid-sentence. "Buy the horse's mother and sisters and brothers. Don't worry about the expense — I'll pay the bill." Then he canceled a multi-million dollar deal to fly to America to see Caroline receive her present. Among John Jr.'s gifts were a speedboat and a Jeep.

He showed his love in more conventional ways. He attended their school plays and took them to baseball games, which he hated. Once, while Jackie and

Jackie Onassis and her son, John F. Kennedy, Jr. leave St. Francis Xavier Church after wedding ceremony of Maria Shriver and Arnold Schwarzenegger, April 26, 1986.

he were lounging on the *Christina*, she suddenly got up from her chair, walked over and gave him a big kiss. "What's that for?" he asked. "That's because of last night," she replied. Ari had spent the night with John Jr. who had been suffering from a stomach ache.

Jackie did not get along with Ari's children, Christina and Alexander. Both naively hoped their parents would be reconciled. They had suffered through Ari's ten-year affair with Maria Callas and despised her. They were spoiled and indulged and their trust funds made them multimillionaires by the time they were twenty-one. Ari never had spent much time with Cristinia and did not hide his disappointment at never producing a second son. She worried about her unruly hair, large nose and heavy figure. She used amphetamines to control her weight, tranquilizers to control her depression.

Christina eloped with Joseph Bolker, a divorced Los Angeles real estate salesman with four grown children, twenty-eight years her senior. She told her father of the marriage by phone. Furious, he disinherited her. The marriage lasted eight months before Bolker gave in to Onassis and agreed to a divorce.

Nor did Ari approve of his son's romantic involvement with Fiona Thyssen, a divorced baroness with two children, beautiful but nearly old enough to be Alexander's mother. When Ari berated him, Alexander baited his father about Jackie, whom he called "the courtesan." On January 21, 1973, Alexander and a test pilot took off from Athens in one of his father's airplanes. Seconds after they were airborne, the plane banked sharply, cartwheeled and crashed. Rescuers rec-

Jacqueline Kennedy Onassis and Senator Edward M. Kennedy at dedication and unveiling ceremonies of a statue of President John F. Kennedy, at the Massachusetts Statehouse lawn in Boston, May 29, 1990.

ognized Alexander only by his bloodstained monogrammed handkerchief. Surgeons labored for three hours to remove blood clots from his brain. News of the plane crash reached Ari and Jackie in the United States. They flew to his side, but Ari soon realized that it was hopeless. He ordered the doctors to turn off the life-support system, then watched helplessly as his son died minutes later.

Consumed with grief, Onassis could not accept the fact that Alexander's death was an accident. He launched an investigation into the crash, offering a large reward for evidence of foul play. He thought of little else for weeks. Jackie felt like an outsider. The wailing grief of Ari and his relatives was simply beyond the range of her tightly controlled emotions. He wanted to revel in his misery and retreat into the past; she wanted to bury the pain and move ahead. In his need, he turned to Maria Callas.

Mrs. Jacqueline Kennedy Onassis walks with Christina Onassis, followed behind by
Senator Edward M. Kennedy, as they leave their plane at Aktion Airport, March 18, 1975.
They accompanied the body of Greek shipping magnate Aristotle Onassis to Skorpios from Paris.

Jacqueline Kennedy Onassis arrives with her daughter, Caroline Kennedy, to attend the wedding of Courtney Kennedy, June 14, 1980 in Washington, D.C. Caroline was one of 13 bridesmaids.

A packet of letters created a pack of troubles in February of 1970. Somehow a New York autograph dealer had been given all the letters Jackie had written to Roswell Gilpatric. The contents of the letters found their way into the newspapers. One, which began "Dearest Roz," had been written from the *Christina* on her honeymoon. It crushed Ari. "My God, what a fool I have made of myself," he told his friends. "I'm afraid my wife is a calculating woman, cold-hearted and shallow."

The day after the letters appeared in the papers, Mrs. Gilpatric filed separation papers on the sixty-three-year-old lawyer. Onassis was humiliated. He no longer cared if they were lovers or not, he felt like a fool. He was not accustomed to having his manhood questioned or laughed at. Jackie was afraid to face him, and told her friends that he would probably divorce her. When she called to explain and apologize, however, Ari told her that all was well and not to worry. He understood perfectly. Only his closest Greek friends knew that the "Dearest Roz" letter was the beginning

of the end of their marriage.

Soon after reassuring Jackie, Onassis was seen in Paris on four separate evenings leaving Maria Callas's apartment at 1 a.m. A few months later he went to the island where she was staying and gave her a pair of antique earrings. A photograph of them kissing appeared in European and American newspapers. Jackie saw the photograph while she was on a plane bound for Greece. A few nights later she and Ari dined at Maxime's in Paris and looked happy. But Ari was no longer a happy man.

Jackie returned to New York and Ari took a long cruise with his daughter. Although he was skeptical about women in business, he now had no choice but to train her to take over. He began taking her to meetings and sent her to New York to work with his ship and insurance brokers. Christina responded well at first and curtailed her aimless social life. But she continued to have bouts of depression and began to feel she could no longer cope with anything. While in London, she took an overdose of sleeping pills and was rushed to

Jacqueline Kennedy Onassis and Christina Onassis, make their way amid crowds of reporters late Feb. 6th, 1975, to enter the Onassis apartment building on fashionable Avenue Foch after they flew from Athens to escort the ailing multimillionaire for medical treatment.

the hospital.

Christina had barely recovered when her mother, Tina Niarchos, died in Paris from an edema of the lung. She blamed her stepfather, Stavros, who in turn said Tina had never recovered from the shock of Christina's attempted suicide. Christina later unsuccessfully sued Niarchos for the $300 million he had inherited from her mother.

Onassis could not bring himself to attend his ex-wife's funeral. He felt old and tired. He had difficulty keeping his eyes open and could not talk without slurring. His ailment was diagnosed as myasthenia gravis, a defect in the body's chemistry that impedes the connection of nerves and muscles. The only evidence of the disease was his drooping eyelids, which had to be taped to his eyebrows to keep his eyes open. He hid the tape behind dark glasses. The doctors feared the disease would weaken his heart.

Ari began staying out late drinking with his friends. Instead of returning to Jackie's apartment, he would go to his suite at the Hotel Pierre and sleep until noon.

"He did not really want to live any more," said Costa Gratsos, an old friend. "He felt cheated. And he blamed himself for having been cheated. He felt responsible for Alexander's death. But there was no self-pity at all. There was an extraordinary degree of stoicism in the way he took everything."

His business was beginning to go bad. The Arab oil embargo nearly crippled his tanker business. Olympic Airways had been steadily losing money.

He had spent time and money lobbying to build an oil refinery in New Hampshire, but the state legislature turned him down. When Jackie suggested they build a house in Acapulco, he said no. He implied that her request was a new form of bloodletting.

Jackie screamed that he was hateful for suggesting such a thing. She bitterly reminded him what her marriage had done to her image at home and abroad. She said she had willingly signed away the right to her full portion of his estate. She did not want his goddamned money now, and she never did want it.

Stung, Onassis rewrote his will, making Christina

World heavyweight boxing champ Muhammad Ali shakes hands with Jacqueline Kennedy Onassis as they meet at a pre-game bash in New York, at the annual Robert F. Kennedy Pro-Celebrity Tennis Tournament.

Jacqueline Kennedy Onassis extends herself to press some flesh at "the market" in New York City's Spanish Harlem, March 24, 1980, while campaigning for Senator Edward M. Kennedy.

Jacqueline Kennedy, followed by Peter Lawford, holds on to John-John on their arrival in Honolulu to begin a vacation. They are preceded down the ramp by Peter Lawford's children, Christopher and Sydney.

Jackie with Edward Kennedy at Harvard.

his major beneficiary and creating a foundation in honor of his late son. He limited Jackie's share of the estate to $150,000 a year for life, plus the same amount to both of her children for the rest of their lives. Aware that Jackie might challenge the will, he wrote:

"I command the executors of my will and the rest of my heirs that they deny her such a right through all legal means, cost and expenses charged to my inheritance." If her legal challenge were to succeed, he decreed that she was to receive no more than 12.5 percent of the total estate, the least he was allowed to leave her under Greek law.

Ari's health began to deteriorate drastically, and he received cortisone treatments to keep the myasthenia gravis under control. What energy he had was focused on the $95 million development of Olympic Towers, a fifty-two-story building overlooking St.

Patrick's Cathedral. He no longer kept up the pretense of his marriage. He stayed at the Pierre; she at her apartment. Encouraged by his daughter, he decided to explore the possibility of divorce.

Roy Cohn, once Senator Joseph McCarthy's chief investigator, was retained as his divorce attorney. A private detective was hired to follow Jackie to see if he could get evidence of adultery. While Ari was secretly arranging for a divorce, Jackie was telling friends that her husband was sick and cranky and hard to deal with but that the marriage was still in good shape.

In the fall, Jackie took the children to Newport for the America's Cup races. She returned to New York and resumed her routine. She bought her winter wardrobe from Valentino and purchased a $200,000 estate in Bernardsville in the New Jersey fox-hunting country. She joined a committee to save Grand Central

Station. She lent her name to various benefits and charities. She jogged, visited her dermatologist, had her hair done at Kenneth's.

Onassis wanted to publicly humiliate Jackie by building a case that would justify the divorce. He told syndicated columnist Jack Anderson evidence of Jackie's profligate spending. Ari then cut her monthly allowance from $30,000 to $20,000 and refused to give her any additional money. He felt that she was taking him for all he was worth; she felt he was victimizing her by withdrawing the money. They began to quarrel bitterly. She now refused to wear the jewelry he gave her. To him the jewels were a way of showing the world what he could afford, and the next time she asked him for money, he suggested she sell her jewelry. She began staying away from him as much as possible.

Onassis was in Greece; Jackie was in New York, partying. She made a public appearance on behalf of the Committee to Save Grand Central Station. A few days later, she received a call from Athens that her husband had collapsed with pains in his abdomen. Accompanied by a heart specialist, she flew from New York to Greece and went directly to Ari's home in Glyfada. The doctor said he should be hospitalized and she agreed. Ari's sisters wanted to keep him at home with specialists in attendance. Jackie insisted he be taken to the American Hospital outside Paris. "He's my husband and I believe this switch is necessary," she said. "Let's not argue."

Arriving in Paris, Ari refused to be carried from the plane on a stretcher. He also insisted on spending the night at his Avenue Foch apartment. From there he talked on the phone to Maria Callas. In the morning he entered the hospital. For five weekends he lay semiconscious, fed intravenously and on a respirator. Doctors performed gall bladder surgery. His blood was replaced every forty-eight hours. His sisters and daughters stayed with him around the clock. For the first several days Jackie was in attendance, but the friction between her and his family became so unbearable that she cut back on her visits.

She began seeing her Paris friends. Paul Mathias took her to see the Peggy Guggenheim art collection. They dined out frequently and took long walks together. She was photographed having dinner with the president of Air France. She shopped for clothes and

Jackie Kennedy Onassis with Gloria Steinem.

The John F. Kennedy Library was announced officially reopened at rededication ceremonies attended by President Clinton with Jacqueline Kennedy Onassis and her children John, Jr. and Caroline, Oct. 29, 1993, in Boston.

Frank Sinatra escorts Jacqueline Kennedy Onassis into New York's 21 Club. Mrs. Onassis had earlier attended Sinatra's concert at the Uris Theater.

had her hair done. Pictures of Jackie enjoying Paris while Onassis lay dying infuriated Christina.

By the end of the month Onassis rallied a bit. He was put on a dialysis machine to relieve his failing kidneys, and put in an oxygen tent to relieve the strain on his lungs. Doctors speculated that he could linger that way for weeks, perhaps months. Jackie decided to fly home to see the children. Ari did not object. Assuming that Jackie would be back after the weekend, Christina agreed to allow Maria Callas one final farewell visit to her father's bedside.

Jackie phoned on Monday. Told that Ari's condition was unchanged, she decided to stay in New York. Later in the week he contracted pneumonia and began slipping away. Still Jackie did not fly back. On Saturday, March 19, 1975, Onassis died with Christina at his side.

Chapter 10

Public opinion turned against Jackie. She was a widow again, but the country did not share her mourning. And no one could fathom why she had left her husband in the hospital to die alone. Her aide, Nancy Tuckerman, tried to put a good face on it. "There was an agreement with Ari that she could spend part of the time with him and part of the time with her children," she told the press. "He wanted it that way. And at this time she just felt she should be with John and Caroline."

Jackie did not want to face the Onassis family alone. Dressed completely in black, she left with her mother for Paris. Teddy Kennedy followed with her children. She was met at the Paris airport by the family chauffeur, who drove her to the Onassis apartment. She stayed there for ten hours before going to the hospital to see her husband's casket. There a family aide told her that Christina could not see her because she was under sedation and resting.

She offered to help arrange the funeral, but was told that everything had been done. Onassis had asked to be buried on Skorpios next to his son with a simple Greek Orthodox service. Jackie went to the chapel at the American Hospital to pay her last respects to her husband. There were no tears, no final kiss good-bye. She bowed her head, said a brief prayer and departed. She smiled at the photographers waiting outside.

The next day she flew with Onassis's body to Greece, where she was met by Christina and escorted to a waiting limousine. Senator Kennedy and her children were in the back seat. Watching Jackie smile at the photographers proved too much for Christina, who had spent the last forty-eight hours watching her father die. Christine bolted from the limousine and joined her aunts in another car.

Jackie was forced to walk behind the Onassis family at the graveside. She stood in the back with her mother, Teddy and the children. After the service Christine went aboard the yacht that bore her name and spoke to the crew. "This boat and this island are mine," she said. "You are all my people now." Teddy tried to speak to her about her father's will, but she cut him off, saying, "You better speak to my lawyers."

After spending the night in Athens, Jackie gave reporters a statement before leaving for Paris. "Aristotle Onassis rescued me at a moment when my life was engulfed with shadows," she said. "He meant a lot to me. He brought me into a world where one could find both happiness and love. We lived through many beautiful experiences together which cannot be forgotten, and for which I will be eternally grateful."

She said her ties with the Onassis family were still close. "Nothing has changed," she said, "both with Aristotle's sisters and his daughter, Christina. The same love binds us as when he lived." She told the reporters that she wanted her children "to be brought up in Greece amidst Greek culture." She was asked about reports that she and Christina were quarreling over the will. "I'll answer that with something my husband told me. Throughout the world people love fairy tales and especially those related to the lives of the rich. You must learn to understand this and accept it."

In New York her lawyers retained Greek counsel to find out what she was entitled to from the Onassis estate. One newspaper had her inheriting $120 million, another $250 million. Publication of the will, however, revealed that Ari left Jackie $100,000 a year in income, plus $50,000 for her children. The bulk of the estate was left to Christina.

Christina was determined to fight any future claim Jackie might make on the estate. The will specified the island and the yacht would be jointly owned by his widow and his daughter. Christina ordered her lawyers to buy Jackie out. She never wanted to deal with her again. The first offer was for $8 million. Jackie said she would accept nothing less than $20 million, plus an addition $6 million in compensation to pay U.S. taxes on the settlement. Christina agreed on the condition that Jackie break all ties with the Onassis family and abandon any further claim to their estate.

Newspapers headlined Jackie's settlement. The Kennedys refused to comment. A year later, Constantine Gratsos, head of the Onassis empire, was asked about Jackie. "Please don't talk to me about that woman," he replied. "She's despicable. I can't bring myself to even think about her. . . And don't even try to see Christina, because she can't bear the thought of that woman. She will turn you down flat. She never wants to see her again, or hear her name. And you must admit she's paid dearly for that one consideration."

Christina, while visiting New York in 1980, attempted to commit suicide by taking a half bottle of

Jackie switches on the lights during opening ceremonies of the renovated Grand Central Terminal in New York. Historic preservation was among her most cherished philanthropic pursuits.

Jacqueline Kennedy Onassis presents the Freedom of Expression in Theater Award to attorney Floyd Abrams at the Municipal Arts Society of New York City's meeting at St. Bartholomew's church in New York.

Jacqueline Kennedy Onassis and Senator Edward M. Kennedy embrace as they pose for photographers following the wedding of her daughter Caroline to Edwin Schlossberg at Our Lady of Victory Church, Centerville, Mass, July 19, 1986.

barbiturates. In 1985 she was married for the fourth time to Thierry Roussel, the heir to a French pharmaceutical fortune, who fathered her only child. They were divorced after three years, and he reportedly received a settlement of $75 million. On November 19, 1988, while visiting friends in Argentina, Christina suffered pulmonary edema and was pronounced dead on arrival at a hospital. She was buried on Skorpios, next to the little chapel, beside her father and brother.

"After Onassis's death, Jackie's great struggle was the need to forge a new identity for herself," recalled her friend Franklin D. Roosevelt, Jr. "She no longer wanted to be known as the wife of a former President of the United States, or the wife of one of the wealthi-

est men on earth. Finally, she wanted to be recognized on the strength of her own merits; she wanted to achieve success, but in her own way and on her own terms."

Six months after the funeral, Tish Baldridge, her former White House social secretary, suggested that Jackie consider publishing as a possible career. Jackie expressed interest, and Tish made several appointments for her, including one with Thomas H. Guizburg, publisher of Viking Press and a family friend of the Bouviers. "I recognized at once what a boon she could be to a publishing firm," he recalled. "She had access to a wide range of interesting and important figures. She knew literally everyone, and in publishing it's not so much what you know but whom you know."

After several meetings, they agreed that Jackie would begin work in September 1975 as a $10,000-a-year, four-days-a-week, consulting editor at Viking. She was assigned an assistant, but her office was small, containing only a desk, chair and telephone. An editor who worked with her, Barbara Burn, said: "Before she came, everybody at Viking was reasonably skeptical. After she arrived, we were all pleasantly surprised that she wasn't a stuffed shirt with a funny voice . . . She was really very serious about what she did."

Jackie had her share of problems at Viking. One of the first books she worked on, *Remember the Ladies: Women of America, 1750 -1815* became a scandal. After the book was published, an article in *Ms.* gave Jackie much credit for the book, provoking the author to publicly deny the extent of Jackie's involvement. After things settled down, though, she made important contributions to a number of books, including *In the Russian Style*, a handsome coffee-table book by Diana Vreeland, the former editor of *Vogue*.

Hugh Auchincloss died in November 1976, and Jackie attended the funeral in Newport. Her stepfather had lost most of his money and Merrywood and Hammersmith Farm had to be sold. Her mother was able to keep the twelve-room former servants' quarters at the farm. Jackie secretly established a million-dollar trust fund for her mother, enabling her to live in comparative ease.

In February 1977, Edith Beale, eighty-one, fell ill and was taken to Southampton Hospital and placed in a small airless room. When Jackie heard this, she commanded: "Get Auntie Edith the best room in the house, and send Nancy Tuckerman the bills." Edith died three days later.

Later that year, Viking published a book called *Shall We Tell the President?*, a novel depicting "President" Edward Kennedy as the target of an assassin. Reviewing the book in The New York Times, John Leonard said: "There is a word for such a book. The word is trash. Anybody associated with its publication should be ashamed of herself." The comment was obviously aimed at Jackie. In truth, she had nothing to do with the book. When Viking issued a statement hinting that had Jackie objected, they would not have published the book, she resigned.

Jackie was not unemployed long. John Sargent, chairman of Doubleday Books, an old friend and occasional escort, asked her to join the company as an associate editor. One inducement was that Nancy

Tuckerman already was working there. They would work together for another fifteen years.

Her early months there received mixed reviews. "Many of the editors resented her," said one of her associates. "We were all handling as many as fifteen books at a time—too much work for too little pay. Jackie took on as few books as she pleased. She was paid full-time, but worked part-time. What's more she had assistants, secretaries, "gofers", telephone ladies working for her." Another said, "She was basically there to bring in celebrities . . . I had the feeling she wasn't getting major stuff done, but she began to do much better later on."

While her colleagues were initially awed by having Jackie in their midst, she soon charmed them by handing out Tootsie Rolls, sitting cross-legged on her office floor to study manuscripts and munching on raw carrots and cucumber sandwiches at her desk. She edited about a dozen books a year and they reflected her eclectic tastes. She edited picture books on art, dance, French and Russian history as well as children's books and best-sellers by Bill Moyers and Michael Jackson.

The authors with whom Jackie worked spoke admiringly of her curiosity, her interest in their work and her great attention to detail. Jonathan Cott, who published several books on Egypt with her, told *The New York Times*: "She was intelligent and passionate about the material; she was an ideal reader and an ideal editor." In a rare interview she told the trade magazine *Publishers Weekly*: "One of the things I like about publishing is that you don't promote the editor—you promote the book and the author."

In a different way, Jackie herself was a publishing phenomena. She has been the subject of twenty-two biographies, and has more listings in the *Readers' Guide to Periodical Literature* than any other living American woman. She appeared on the cover of the *Ladies' Home Journal* sixteen times, on *McCall's* thirteen times. "She was our Lady Di," said Ellen Levine, the editor of *Redbook*. "I would have killed for an interview. Ultimately, I respect her for never giving it."

She was the subject of a feature film and four television miniseries. The 1978 feature, The Greek Tycoon, cost Anthony Quinn, who played Onassis in the film, Jackie's friendship. Jackie was portrayed by Jacqueline Bisset. In the 1991 miniseries *A Woman Named Jackie*, the title role was played by Irish actress Roma Downey. In the 1981 miniseries *Jacqueline Bouvier Kennedy*, Jackie was played by Jaclyn Smith, a former angel in *Charlie's Angels*. Francesca Annis was Jackie in *Onassis*, a miniseries in 1988. Blair Brown,

Jacqueline Kennedy Onassis, her daughter Caroline (right) and Senator Edward M. Kennedy applaud the sculptress who created a statue of President John F. Kennedy for the Massachusetts Statehouse lawn in Boston at dedication and unveiling ceremonies, May 29, 1990.

who most closely resembled Jackie, played her in the 1983 miniseries *Kennedy*.

By now, Jackie was back in the good graces of the Kennedy clan. She had supported Sargent Shriver's ill-fated run for the Presidency in 1976 and contributed $25,000 to his campaign. She supported a textile factory in the Bedford-Stuyvesant section of Brooklyn because the project had been important to Bobby Kennedy. She arranged for Caroline to work a summer in Senator Kennedy's office. John worked with Sargent Shriver's children on an overseas poverty project. She was an honorary chairman of a benefit at the Kennedy Center in Washington. She spent more time at Hyannisport.

A lot of Jackie's time was spent with her children. It is not easy to be a rich child. For the Kennedy children, the problems were multiplied. Every time they went out, they were prey. An offhand comment could end up in the newspapers. The natural reaction should have been rebellion. Others rebelled. A few of Caroline and John Jr.'s cousins were especially ungracious and self destructive. Jackie worked hard at giving her children values. She did not confine or restrict them. But somehow both children developed moral compasses that kept them from crossing the line into danger. They are well adjusted, not only by the standards of the Kennedys, but by any standards.

There was no secret formula. She did it with love, commitment, hands-on supervision, respect for learning, for accomplishment and for the feelings of others. She also passed along her sense of humor and irreverence. She was not just Caroline and John Jr.'s mother, she was their friend.

Caroline Kennedy, like her mother, grew up to be a private person. She chose not to undergo the ritual of a debutante party, and she deferred college to enroll in an art program in London. Caroline attended Radcliffe and did well in her studies, like her mother. During the summer following her sophomore year, she was a copygirl on the New York Daily News. After her graduation in 1980, she moved into a New York apartment with friends and took a job in the film and tele-vision office of the Metropolitan Museum of Art.

Raising John was more difficult. Fatherless and without direction, John was subjected to a "toughening up" program devised and implemented by his mother. She asked a Secret Service agent to give John boxing lessons. He punched out a secondary school classmate for calling him John-John. After school one day, he pelted a newspaper photographer with snowballs.

At age eleven he was sent to the Drake Island Adventure Center at Plymouth, England, for a "week-long course for young people in sailing, canoeing, climbing and character development." At thirteen he participated in the rugged Outward Bound program. He was given still another "rite of passage," a seventy-day survival course supervised by the National Outdoor Leadership School.

Worried about John's academic progress, Jackie enrolled him at Phillips Academy in Andover, Massachusetts, where he enjoyed acting in school plays. He attended Brown University, graduating in 1983, and participated in a work-study program in India. Both Caroline and John became lawyers.

Janet Auchincloss surprised her daughters by remarrying. Bingham Morris, a retired investment banker from Southampton, Long Island, had been married to Mary Rawlins, a bridesmaid at Janet's wedding to Black Jack Bouvier. When Mary died, he began courting Janet, and they were married in a small ceremony in Newport.

Jackie decided to build for herself a nineteen-room Cape Cod-style house and an adjoining six-room guest house on 275 acres of oceanfront property in the village of Gay Head on Martha's Vineyard. Problems developed during construction. Jackie was constantly making changes. A barn and a silo, which was to be John's quarters, were built about 200 feet from the house. The silo exceeded the maximum height imposed by the local building codes, and it had to be lowered by three feet. When it was finally finished in 1981, it had cost Jackie roughly $3.5 million.

Chapter 11

One of her first guests at the Martha's Vineyard house was Maurice Tempelsman. He had known Jackie for years; first as a friend, later as her financial advisor, and more recently as her companion. Her friends believed that in Maurice she had found the peace of mind she had sought so long. "I admire Maurice's strength and his success," she said. "I hope my notoriety doesn't force him out of my life."

Tempelsman was an unlikely beau for Jackie. He was born in 1929 into an Orthodox Jewish family in Antwerp, Belgium, that fled Europe in 1940 to escape Hitler. After two years on the island of Jamaica, the Tempelsmans arrived in New York. By age fifteen, Maurice was working for his father, a diamond broker, and taking night courses in business administration at New York University. When he was twenty-one, he convinced U.S. government officials to buy industrial diamonds for its stockpile of strategic materials maintained for national emergencies. He made millions as the middleman.

His deals made him a familiar figure in Washington circles. Adlai Stevenson was his attorney. He became an associate of Harry Oppenheimer, owner-and director of deBeers, the world's largest distributors of diamonds. Along the way he befriended a number of emerging African leaders.

Tempelsman became friends with Jackie in the late 1950s. He and Oppenheimer made large contributions to Kennedy's campaign. He and his wife, Lily, were frequent guests at the White House. Like Onassis, Tempelsman was short, portly and looked older than his age. They both smoked cigars, collected art and had a love of the sea, although his yacht, the sixty-five-foot *Ralemar*, was not in a class with Onassis's *Christina*. Both had the gift of making money. Jackie entrusted to Tempelsman the $20 million she had received from Christina Onassis. Through shrewd investments her assets ballooned more than $100 million.

Jackie and Maurice spent a lot of time together. He squired her around New York. They cruised on the *Ralemar*, spent weekends at her farm in Bernardsville, New Jersey, where she rode horses, and vacationed in Martha's Vineyard. He never accompanied her when she made a round of political appearances in support of Ted Kennedy's 1980 run for the Democratic Party presidential nomination.

A cousin of Tempelsman, Rose Schreiber, said that if Jackie married her first husband for status and her second for money, then her attachment to Maurice was based on mutual respect and friendship. "Although Maurice appears to be meek and unassuming, he is a charming, worldly figure," she explained. "He dresses well, likes to read, loves to travel and go to the opera. He has savoir faire. He also enjoys the simple pleasures that nature has to offer . . . Women have always been attracted to him."

Maurice had a marital problem. His wife, Lily, whom he married when they were twenty, was a strict Orthodox Jew. Divorce was not an alternative for Lily, although in November 1980 she took the initiative and asked Maurice to leave. They separated on friendly terms, but remained married. He moved into a hotel suite, spending several nights a week at Jackie's apartment. Finally, he moved in with her.

For years, Jackie and Maurice refrained from public displays of affection. They never held hands or walked arm-in-arm, and took great pains to avoid kissing when their picture could be taken. When he first visited her on Martha's Vineyard, he would dock his boat and enter her house through the oceanside backyard," so he wouldn't be photographed.

Caroline became involved with Edwin Schlossberg, who like Maurice, came from an Orthodox Jewish background. His father was the founder and president of Alfred Schlossberg, Inc., a New York textile company, the president of Congregation Rodeph Sholom and a major supporter of Jewish and Zionist causes. The Schlossbergs had a second home in Palm Beach.

Edwin was a scholar with a Ph. D. in science and literature from Columbia University, and had taught for awhile at Southern Illinois University. He had been one of the developers of the Brooklyn Children's Museum.

Caroline met Schlossberg at a dinner party in 1981 and invited him to her mother's Christmas party. Jackie liked his looks—he was tall, husky and prematurely grey—and introduced him to her guests as "my daughter's new friend, Ed Schlossberg." He represented a new direction for Caroline. She found him witty, bright and supportive. In 1984, when her cousin, David Kennedy, twenty-eight, was found dead of a drug overdose in a Palm Beach motel, it was Schlossberg who

On the town in London, at the famous Claridge's Hotel.

President Bill Clinton speaks with Jacqueline Kennedy Onassis, widow of late President John F. Kennedy at the rededication ceremony of the Kennedy Presidential Library in Boston, Oct. 29, 1993.

helped Caroline out of her depression.

Schlossberg had a good effect on Caroline. She lost weight and began to dress with some of her mother's flair. She became a member of the trustees of the John F. Kennedy Library. She left her job at the Metropolitan Museum in 1985 to enroll at the Columbia University School of Law. A year later, John Jr. enrolled at the New York University Law School. Jackie was delighted that both her children would have legal careers.

The engagement was announced in March 1986. The wedding was held in July at the Church of Our Lady of Victory, Centerville, Massachusetts. There was no Catholic mass, neither was a rabbi present. Caroline wore a white satin organza gown with a twenty-five foot train, designed for her by Carolina Herrera. There were 425 guests, of whom twenty-one were the groom's. A security force of more than a hundred kept the press and the spectators at bay.

After a month-long honeymoon in Hawaii and Japan, the newlyweds settled down in a luxurious Park Avenue apartment.

In the spring of 1988, Jackie was telling friends, "I'm going to be a grandmother—imagine that." On June 25th, Caroline gave birth to a 7-pound, 12-ounce girl. She was named Rose after Caroline's grandmother, who was a month away from her ninety-eighth birthday. Jackie reportedly was a nervous wreck waiting for her granddaughter to arrive. John Jr. kept telling his mother to "cool out." Caroline yielded to family pressure and agreed to raise her child as a Catholic.

Two years later, Caroline gave birth to another daughter, Tatiana, and in 1993, a boy, John Bouvier Kennedy. The press now was calling the proud grandmother "Granny O." She often would walk the ten blocks to the Schlossberg apartment and take over. In good weather, she would take the children to Central Park, where she was just another grandma out for a stroll. She, Rose and Tatiana would ride the carousel, and she would buy them ice cream. If the children wandered away, Jackie would let out a loud Indian -whoop and they'd come running back.

Jackie increasingly looked to her grandchildren to add light and joy to her life. She loved to baby-sit them once a week. "She was so wonderful with them," says her friend Rose Styron, the wife of writer William Styron. "She got such a kick out of watching them tumble and play together. On the day she died, she and friends looked at last year's snapshots from Jackie's Labor Day picnic on Martha's Vineyard and reminisced

about teaching little Jack to sing "Itsy Bitsy Spider."

Things were going well with John Jr., too. He made a striking appearance introducing his uncle, Senator Ted Kennedy at the 1988 Democratic National Convention in Atlanta. People Magazine named him "The Sexiest Man Alive." He completed law school, passed the bar on his third try, and became an assistant prosecutor in the office of Manhattan District Attorney Robert Morganthau. He was romantically linked with movie actress Daryl Hannah.

Jackie had always enjoyed good health, and she seemed set for a happy old age. In February 1994, however, she announced that she was undergoing treatment for non-Hodgkin's lymphoma. Doctors said they believed they had caught the disease in its early stages, and began chemotherapy. As the months passed, they remained optimistic, calling her prognosis excellent, even after she underwent emergency surgery for a bleeding ulcer on April 14. But while some lymphomas can be left untreated for years, nearly half can kill within months. The disease claims some 21,000 victims a year.

Discharged from the hospital six days later, Jackie returned to the life she loved. She worked with authors at Doubleday, played with her grandchildren, even went to a screening of the movie Schindler's List.

Lymphoma gets its name from the lymphocytes, or white blood cells, it infects. These cells normally course through the bloodstream and lymph system, a network of small glands concentrated in the neck, groin and armpits. Healthy lymphocytes proliferate only as needed to combat viruses or bacteria. Cancerous ones proliferate endlessly, crowding out healthy cells. At first, lymphoma may cause no symptoms other than a swollen gland like the one Jackie felt in December 1993.

Jackie's cancer didn't respond to treatment. It spread to her spinal cord in just two months. Drugs were injected directly into her brain through a tube in her skull, but the cancer soon invaded her liver.

She could be seen walking with Maurice in Central Park as best she could, passing the places where she played as a child, a cap covering the hair loss caused by chemotherapy. Maurice stood by as the disease ravaged her body, hoping to counter the indignities of the medical process with kindness. "He would help her into the examining room, help her walk to the ladies' room," recalled a hospital attendant. "He was always holding her hand or caressing her cheek."

In April, she told a friend, Countess Isabelle d'Ornano, that things were going well: "I'm almost glad it happened because it's given me a second life. I laugh and enjoy things so much more." The reassuring words did not fool the Countess: "She knew she was lost," She was hospitalized on May 16 with what doctors called serious complications of her cancer. Two days later, at her request, John Jr. and Caroline escorted their mother home. Teddy Kennedy flew in from Washington. Her parish priest, Monsignor Georges Bardes of the Church of St. Thomas More, arrived to hear her confession and give her the last rites.

On the morning of May 20, John, Jr. stood in front of the apartment where he and Caroline had been raised and made a brief statement to the hundreds of reporters, cameramen and well-wishers who had gathered there. "Last night, at around 10:15, my mother passed on," he said. "She was surrounded by her friends and family and her books and the people and things that she loved. And she did it in her own way, and we all feel lucky for that, and now she's in God's hand."

"There's been an enormous outpouring of good wishes from everyone in both New York and beyond," he added. "And I speak for all our family when we say we're extremely grateful. And I hope now that, you know, we can just have these next couple of days in relative peace."

But onlookers continued to arrive. They jostled for space behind police barricades. On Sunday, when John Jr. emerged onto the fourteenth-floor balcony to wave to the well-wishers, some shouted to him, "We love Jackie." Others broke into a spontaneous rendition of "God Bless America."

Inside the apartment, the Kennedy children planned their mother's funeral. They ordered white peonies for the altar at St. Ignatius Loyola church on Park Avenue, chose the readings, and personally called or sent hand-delivered invitations to some 700 family members, political figures and friends. "Three things came to mind," recalled John Jr. of the process of arranging a suitable service. "They were her love of words, the bonds of home and family, and her spirit of adventure."

On Monday, May 23, outside the church where Jackie was baptized and confirmed, police kept thousands of onlookers at a distance while guests filed in. They included her sister, Lee Radziwill Ross, Hillary Rodham Clinton, former First Lady Bird Johnson, New York Mayor Rudolph Giuliani, Yoko Ono, Carly Simon, Mike Nichols and Diane Sawyer.

The Reverend Walter Modrys, the pastor of St. Ignatius, officiated during the eighty-minute ceremony. John Jr. read from the Book of Isaiah, Caroline recited one of her mother's favorite Edna St. Vincent Millay poems. Maurice Tempelsman read "Ithaka" by the Greek poet C. P. Cavafy, and bid his companion a sad farewell. "And now the journey is over," he said, "too short, alas, too short."

Opera diva Jessye Norman sang Franck's "Panis Angelicus" and Shubert's "Ava Maria." Senator Kennedy gave the eulogy. "She never wanted public notice," he said, "in part, I think, because it brought painful memories of an unbearable sorrow, endured the glare of public lights."

Outside, a press helicopter hovered above the church. Some mourners in the crowd cried, some made the sign of the cross, others listened to the mass on their radios, reciting along with the service and singing along with the hymns.

At 12:45 p.m., her body was transported on a chartered 737 Boeing jet from New York to Washington, where a motorcade of motorcycles, buses and limousines escorted Jackie through the black iron gates of Arlington National Cemetery. A private gathering of fewer than a hundred people, including President and Mrs. Clinton, watched as Jackie, in a mahogany casket covered with ferns and a cross of white lilies-of-the-valley, was laid to rest between her husband Jack and her stillborn daughter. Her son Patrick lies on the other side of the President.

"God gave her very great gifts and imposed upon her great burdens," said President Clinton during the eleven-minute ceremony. "She bore them all with dignity and grace and uncommon common sense."

As Jackie's friends and family knelt to touch the coffin a final time, filing past the eternal flame that she herself first lit three decades ago, sixty-four bells rang out from the Washington National Cathedral across the Potomac, one for each year of her extraordinary life. Then the black limousines drove out the gates, and the crowds began to scatter. An era had ended.

Mother and son make a handsome pair at a Boston fundraiser for the Kennedy Library.

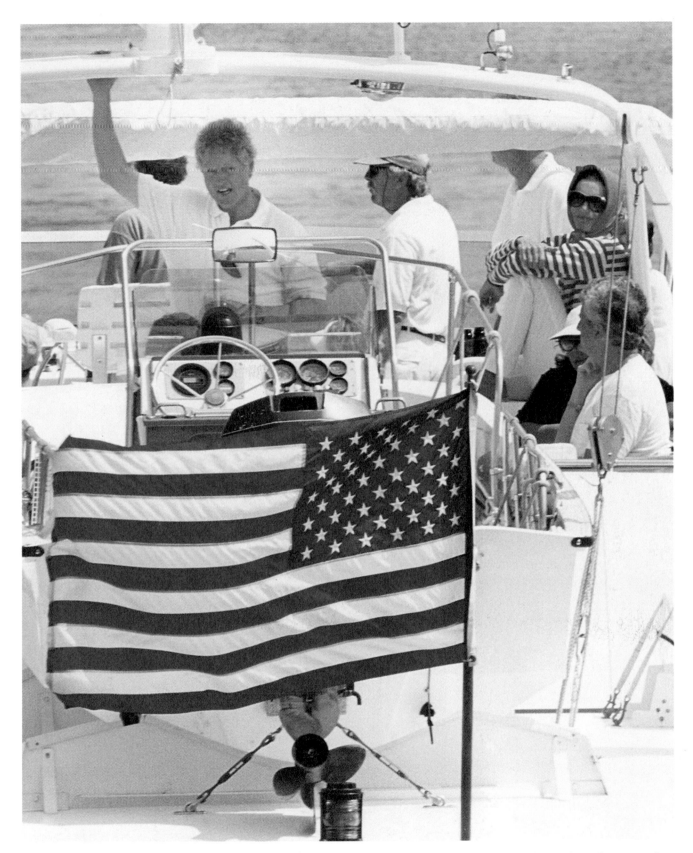

President Clinton and former First Lady Jacqueline Kennedy Onassis (r) enjoy a cruise on the yacht Relemar in the waters off Martha's Vineyard, August 24th, 1993.

Jacqueline Kennedy Onassis smiling with Senator Edward M. Kennedy and her children John F. Kennedy, Jr. and Caroline Kennedy Schlossberg as Connecticut Governor Lowell Weicker accepts the 1992 John F. Kennedy Profile in Courage Award from the Kennedy family at the John F. Kennedy Presidential Library in Boston, May 28, 1993.

Jacqueline Kennedy Onassis' steady companion, Maurice Templesman, mournfully departing her apartment house following her death.

Funeral home staff carry the body of Jacqueline Kennedy Onassis, the wife of former U.S. President John F. Kennedy, from St. Ignatius Catholic Church in New York, May 23, 1994.

A dramatic portrait of the media frenzy that engulfed Jacqueline Onassis' death. Here the Kennedy children are surrounded while attempting to enter their late mother's home.

John F. Kennedy, Jr. and Caroline Kennedy Schlossberg watch as their mother Jacqueline Kennedy Onassis' casket is placed in a hearse outside St. Ignatius Loyola Catholic Church in New York, May 23, 1994, after her funeral.

Caroline Kennedy Schlossberg and her brother John F. Kennedy, Jr. watch as the body of their mother Jacqueline Kennedy Onassis is placed in a hearse outside St. Ignatius Loyola Catholic Church in New York, May 23, 1994, after her funeral. Behind Caroline is her husband, Edwin.

John F. Kennedy, Jr. touches the gravestone of his father, former President John F. Kennedy, at Arlington National Cemetery, May 23, 1994. The casket of Jacqueline Kennedy Onassis sits beside the flame.

Archbishop Philip Hannan presides over the burial of former First Lady Jacqueline Kennedy Onassis, at Arlington National Cemetery, May 23, 1994. She was laid to rest next to her husband, former President John F. Kennedy.

Jacqueline Kennedy Onassis, 1929-1994
In Memory